FACTS ABOUT

FINLAND

OTAVA PUBLISHING COMPANY LTD.
HELSINKI

Principal articles witten by:
PÄIVI ELOVAINIO, Dr. Pol. Sc., Senior lecturer
JUKKA TARKKA, Dr. Pol. Sc.
ALLAN TIITTA, Ph. D., Senior lecturer
KLAUS TÖRNUDD, Dr. pol. Sc.
KAIJA VALKONEN, M. A.
JYRKI VESIKANSA, Lic. Pol.
OSMO A. WIIO, Dr. Soc. Sc.
SEPPO ZETTERBERG, Ph. D., Professor

Updated information
in internet:
http://virtual.finland.fi
http://formin.finland.fi

3rd edition

English translation: Timothy Binham
Graphic design: Katja Alanen
Layout: Eija Hiltunen
Cover design: Maija Vallinoja

Printed by:
Otava Book Printing Co.
Keuruu 2002

ISBN 951-1-18502-0

FACTS ABOUT

FIN-
LAND

Contents

Finland in the World

Like all countries, Finland has many identities and many roles to play in the world. Finland is an industrialized European country, a member state in many international organizations, a Nordic country, and an immediate neighbour of the territorially largest country in the world. In terms of power politics Finland is generally regarded as a "small state", not capable of having a major influence on world affairs. Instead of playing power politics, Finland prefers to work for international cooperation, even integration.

Finland is of course affected by globalization, growing dependence on international exchanges and interaction with other players on the international scene. Therefore, Finland shares many of the same experiences with other countries and displays similar features. This is true whether we talk about climate change and global warming, the effects of rising oil prices, problems of an aging population, the predominance of identical consumer products and many other phenomena, some of them trivial, some of them having important long-range consequences for human societies.

The purpose of the present chapter on Finland in the world is to put in perspective some of the more specific characteristics of Finland as one of the partners in the world arena.

A Nordic country

Finland is known as one of the five Nordic countries, a group that shares common values and also has much of its history in common. The Scandinavian cultural heritage, similar political

◀ Although in 1889 Finland was still a grand duchy of the Russian Empire, it had its own pavilion at the Paris World Fair. Here, Mme Paris receiving the young damsel Finland, who bears a representation of Helsinki Cathedral on her hat. A further symbolic note is added by the parcels in the boat, marked E.U. *(Exposition Universelle).*

systems of parliamentary democracy, shared ideas about civil rights and social welfare as well as many other facts and circumstances explain the natural readiness of Finns to identify with the Nordic region and define their country accordingly. Finland was a part of the kingdom of Sweden until 1809 and retained its Swedish constitution and legal system even during the following century as an autonomous grand duchy in the Russian realm until full independence was achieved in 1917. This has left indelible marks on Finnish society as a whole.

In the modern world, the Nordic countries form a close network of co-operation and interaction. Travel and non-governmental organizations bring together people on the grass roots level, thus forming a natural basis for common official institutions. The principal institutions are the Nordic Council, founded in 1952, and the Nordic Council of Ministers, established in 1971. The Nordic Council is composed of 87 parliamentarians designated by the national parliaments. The self-governing province of Åland has its own representatives within the Finnish delegation to the Nordic Council (in the same way, the Faroe Islands and Greenland have their representatives within the Danish delegation). A large part of the work of the inter-parliamentary Nordic Council is carried out in committees that meet throughout the year. Plenary sessions are held annually, with thematic sessions sometimes arranged in addition to the regular ones. The end products of the work of the Council are mostly detailed recommendations addressed to the Nordic Council of Ministers and thus indirectly to the governments.

For its part, the Nordic Council

ÅLAND

■ Åland has a special status in Finland as a demilitarized and self-governing province. The foundation for the demilitarization of the Åland Islands was laid in the Paris treaty of 1856 that ended the Crimean war. The demilitarized and neutral status of Åland was confirmed and extended in subsequent treaties, in particular the multilateral Åland Convention, concluded in 1921 on the initiative of the League of Nations.

The autonomous status of the province of Åland is also based on a decision of the Council of the League of Nations in 1921 that resolved a dispute over the islands between Finland and Sweden. The self-government of the province is intended to guarantee the preservation of the Swedish language and culture in Åland. It has earned Åland its own representative in the Nordic Council along with representatives of other Nordic self-governing areas, the Faroe Islands and Greenland.

Inside the European Union, Åland benefits from exemptions that have made it possible to retain duty-free shopping in the ferry-boat traffic that connects Finland and Sweden. This is vital for the continuation of reasonably priced ferry communications. The picture shows ferry-boats belonging to the two big passenger ship lines, Silja Line and Viking Line, in the harbour of Mariehamn. In the background the town of Mariehamn and the four-masted museum bark ship Pommern.

▲ The flags of the five Nordic countries:
Sweden, Finland, Norway, Denmark and Iceland.

◀ In 1955 Finland
joined the Nordic
Council, founded by
Denmark, Sweden,
Norway and Iceland
during the Cold War
to deepen inter-
Nordic cooperation
in matters such as
freedom of move-
ment. The NORDEK
free trade area,
however, did not get
off the ground. The
picture shows the
Nordic prime
ministers drawing
up cooperation
proposals.

of Ministers is the central inter-governmental body in charge of Nordic cooperation. It meets at least once a year on the level of prime ministers, often together with the presidium of the Nordic Council. Other meetings are held with sectoral ministers attending. Furthermore, one minister in each Nordic government has the overall duty to oversee the coordination of Nordic cooperation. The decisions of the Nordic Council of Ministers are binding on the governments except when they have specifically opted out from some particular project. The Council of Ministers prepares programmes for cooperation and issues reports to the Nordic Council, in particular about steps taken in order to implement recommenda-

tions adopted by the Nordic Council. The secretariat for the Nordic Council of Ministers is located in Copenhagen.

Originally the substantive fields of Nordic cooperation were grouped into five main categories: cultural, econom-

▲ Sweden's young king Carl XVI Gustav and President Urho Kekkonen used to hunt together.

▼ The citizens of the Nordic countries have close contacts at grassroots level. The Youth League of the Finnish Norden Association runs the Nordjobb exchange, which enables any EU citizen aged 18 to 26 who speaks Danish, Norwegian or Swedish to apply for a summer job in one of the Nordic countries. Nordjobb participants are also offered a varied programme of leisure activities. In the picture, Nordic youths learning how to bake *tikkupulla* buns on an open fire.

ic, legal, social as well as transport and communications. New items such as environment protection are now high on the agenda, while some of the traditional areas of Nordic cooperation have been superseded lately by cooperation and integration on the European level. Nordic cooperation is therefore now organized in three main pillars, focussing on the Nordic region, on Europe and on the "adjacent areas" (meaning the Baltic states and Russia). Among the important achievements of Nordic cooperation may be mentioned the common labour market and passport union established already in 1954, enabling Nordic citizens to move freely and seek employment without passports or work permits, enjoying the same social rights, in all Nordic countries. Since the late 1970's, Nordic citizens resident in other Nordic countries have had the right to vote in local elections. A common Nordic Investment Bank has its headquarters in Helsinki. These and other examples show that Nordic integration has in many ways anticipated arrangements introduced much later in the European Union. The Nordic passport union was incorporated in 2001 into the area covered by the Schengen agreement, which created a wide European passport union.

Particularly during the years of the cold war, Finns set great store by their Nordic identity, making it clear where Finland stood in a world divided between different political systems. This identity was strengthened by wide-ranging Nordic cooperation in foreign policy, which was mostly handled informally, outside the framework of the above-mentioned common Nordic institutions. This cooperation continues on many levels, particularly in the United Nations and other international organizations as well as in international peacekeeping operations and in development cooperation. It is coordinated at the highest level by the foreign ministers at regular meetings.

Finland in Europe

Even in the cold war years, Finland had joined or cooperated with a number of European organizations, but Finland's engagement in European integration only really began to expand in the 1990s. In earlier years, Finland maintained a stance of neutrality and

▼ In 1975, Finland hosted the third stage of the Conference on Security and Co-operation in Europe, which was held in Helsinki at the level of Heads of State or Government. The picture shows President Urho Kekkonen talking with the President of France, Valéry Giscard d'Estaing and the Prime Minister of the United Kingdom, Harold Wilson.

▲ The euro coins introduced into circulation in 2002 have national symbols on one side. The euro coin released in Finland depicts a swan, representing Finnish nature, and the cent a lion, from the country's coat of arms.

1994. A referendum in October the same year gave a result of 57% in favour and 43% against membership. Thus, Finland was able to join the Union as a full member as of January 1995, together with Austria and Sweden. Norway had also negotiated for membership, but the majority of the Norwegians rejected the agreement in their referendum in November 1994. Both Iceland and Norway are, however, members of the European Economic Area and thus included in the EU internal market (excluding the market for agricultural products). Among the Nordic countries, Finland alone is a member of the European Monetary Union, while Denmark and Sweden have remained outside, at least for the time being. Although Denmark has a longer history of membership, Finland is in some important respects more deeply engaged in the integration represented by the European Union than any of the other Nordic countries.

aloofness with respect to some European institutions, but today it is an enthusiastic partner in promoting regional integration in Europe. The European Union is the predominant forum for this, but other organizations such as the Council of Europe and the Organization for Security and Cooperation in Europe should also be mentioned.

Finland applied for EU membership in 1992. After one year of negotiations, agreement was reached in March

▼ Finland joined the European Union in 1995 and the Schengen Area in 2001. The picture shows the passport control points for EU citizens and non-EU citizens in Helsinki's South Harbour terminal.

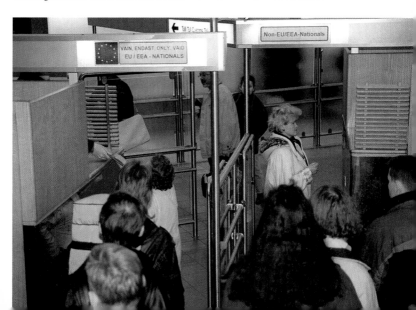

HEIDI HAUTALA

■ Sixteen of the European Parliament's 626 members are Finns. One of them is Heidi Hautala, who has energetically advocated public access to Union documents while championing "green" values. She has been a member of the Green Group of the European Parliament throughout Finland's membership. She is chairman of the EP Greens/European Free Alliance.

Hautala believes that an MEP's influence depends more on initiative and expertise than the size of her or his political group. Successful action requires networking across party lines.

After taking a degree in agriculture and forestry, Hautala edited several journals advocating green values and served as Member of the Finnish Parliament for four years. In 2000 she was a presidential candidate for the Greens.

The motives for the accession of Finland to the EU were both political and economic. It was felt that Finland needed a new and stable attachment to a strong European institution at a time when the threat of confrontation between the two military alliances in Europe, NATO and the Warsaw pact, had receded. Finland did not want to be marginalized and isolated in the new Europe. Joining the European Union was thus clearly perceived as a way of enhancing Finnish security. Economic considerations included the need to surmount the depression of the early 1990s and to have a say in the processes of economic transformation affecting all of Europe.

Agriculture was the principal branch of the Finnish economy that had been outside all schemes of integration in which Finland had previously participated. Joining the EU was therefore a controversial matter for the Finnish farmers (6% of the work force), most of whom voted against joining. The effects of membership have been considerable. Prices of agricultural products were immediately adjusted downwards to conform to European levels. National subsidies to agriculture were supplanted by EU subsidies, and agreements with the EU have enabled specific grants to compensate for the difficulties caused by the short growing season and harsh climate. After all, one of the declared purposes of the EU is to maintain a healthy farm sector and a populated countryside. Nevertheless, adaptation has been difficult. The subsidies have not been sufficient to counteract an ongoing process of change: the number of farms is shrinking, while their size is growing.

The number of EU members is expected to increase considerably by the year 2004, assuming that the current process of preparing agreements of accession with a number of candidate countries proceeds smoothly. This will alter the character of the Union in important respects and require adjustments, for example, to the common agricultural policy. The admission of new members from Central and Eastern Europe will put further strain on

the resources available for agriculture, but for political reasons Finland is nevertheless strongly in favour of expanding the Union. A more broadly based European Union is regarded as an important factor for stability and well-being in the European continent as a whole.

Finland was in charge of the EU presidency during the latter half of 1999. It thus fell to Finland to lead the Union into the new millennium, a task that was taken very seriously, as preparations started already three years earlier. Among the key issues handled during the presidency were the question of enlargement and the development of a common crisis management capability. As regards the internal functioning of the EU, Finland took advantage of the presidency to promote its well-established policies of consumer protection, environmental responsibility and transparency in EU decision-making.

A durable feature of Finnish EU policy is also the Northern Dimension Initiative, which purports to bring

▲ Farming in a cold climate has been the hallmark of life in rural Finland over the centuries. Today, the conditions of agriculture are undergoing rapid transformation: the number of farms is shrinking, and their average size is growing. Finnish agricultural policy aims to keep the countryside vital and support an ecologically sustainable agriculture that offers consumers safe high quality products. In Finland, the soil and air are clean, the livestock is healthy, and the standard of food hygiene is high.
The picture shows a corn-field at Kalajoki, golden in the evening sun.

ERKKI LIIKANEN

■ Erkki Liikanen, European Commissioner for Enterprise and Information Society, speaking on the subject "Knowledge and competence – conditions of success for the European enterprises". Erkki Liikanen has been the Finnish member of the European Commission since 1995. Prior to his current assignment, he was in charge of budget issues, personnel and internal administration in 1995–1999.

In the years 1990–1994 Erkki Liikanen served as Head of Finland's Mission to the European Union. In this capacity he was closely involved in the negotiations that led to Finland's EU membership in 1995. He was elected to the Finnish Parliament in 1972 at the age of 21, representing the Social Democratic party, and in 1987–1990 he served as the Minister of Finance of Finland before his appointment to the Foreign Service.

together EU member states with partner countries in northern Europe for a number of common projects.

Relations with Russia

The presence of Russia has always been strongly felt in Finland. There have been many wars over the centuries between Sweden and Russia, often on Finnish land. As a result of the war that ended in 1809, Finland became an autonomous grand duchy of the Russian Empire. Its new status entailed a Russian military presence and peaceful development under the old Swedish legal system, which Finland was allowed to retain. Attempts at "Russification" and other acts of repression at the end of the 19th century met with resistance and fuelled the independence movement. Shortly after the Russian October revolution, the Finnish Parliament declared Finland an independent republic on 6 December 1917. Relations with Soviet Russia, later the Soviet Union, were severely strained from the outset by warfare between Finnish government forces and nationalists against Finnish and Russian Bolsheviks in 1918–1919 and by lingering mutual suspicion. Connivance between Nazi Germany and the Soviet Union led to the Soviet aggression against Finland in 1939–1940. Squeezed between the dictatorships, Finland fought another war against the Soviet Union during the years 1941–1944, and then against Germany in 1944–1945.

After the second World War, the Finnish government made determined efforts to gain the confidence of the Soviet leadership and to overcome the tensions of the past. Resettlement of the displaced population from the territories ceded to the Soviet Union and the payment of war reparations slowed down post-war recovery, but those tasks were completed by the early 1950s. The Finnish-Soviet relationship developed favourably in many respects, but it was also burdened by interference and pressure from the Soviet side and by inhibitions on the Finnish side. On the grass roots level, nostalgia for the lost territories is still deeply ingrained in the minds of many sectors of the Finnish population.

Relations have developed on a new basis with the sovereign Russian Federation that superseded the Soviet Union as Finland's eastern neighbour in 1992. The problems caused by the presence of a neighbouring expansionist and distrustful dictatorship have disappeared. There is consequently good reason to claim that relations between independent Finland and Russia were never as good before as they have been since the early 1990s. Finland needs a democratic, stable and friendly Russia as its neighbour, and remarkable progress has been made in this direction. Finland's border with Russia, more than 1200 kilometres long, is also the only land border between the European Union and the Russian Federation, representing a wide gap in living standards between the two sides. A visa regime is still in force for travel between the two countries.

After a temporary slowdown in the early 1990s, when Russia was laying the foundations for a market economy, trade between Finland and Russia is flourishing again. Russia is now Finland's fifth trade partner after Germany, Sweden, the United States and the United Kingdom, accounting for about 8% of Finland's total foreign trade. Finland's main imports from Russia

◀ Tourism, trade and transport as well as investments and industrial cooperation play important roles in the evolving relations between Finland and Russia. These relations also include personal contacts on the highest level. During her working visit to St Petersburg, President Tarja Halonen met the President of the Russian Federation Vladimir Putin. The picture shows the two presidents enjoying a walk in the sunshine in May 2002 at Pushkin, near St Petersburg.

are raw materials and energy products (oil, natural gas, electric power). The market for exporting to Russia has become highly competitive, and many smaller firms are nowadays involved in it. Many Finnish companies, for example in the brewery business, have made successful investments in Russian markets.

In 1999, during the German presidency, the European Union adopted a Common Strategy on Russia. As Finland took over the presidency for the second half of the same year, the implementation of this strategy was one of its top priorities. In general terms, Finland is fully associated with the priorities regarding Russian relations to western Europe that have been propounded by the Council of Europe, the European Union, NATO and their member states. One of the principal goals is to integrate Russia as far as possible into the network of institutions charged with maintaining security and stability in the continent of Europe.

The Baltic and the Arctic

Like the Mediterranean in the south, the Baltic Sea is surrounded by a number of countries that are all interested in using the sea – for transport, fishing, recreation and other purposes. The political configuration around the Baltic Sea changed drastically at the beginning of the 1990s with the reunification of Germany, the dissolution of the Soviet Union and the re- emergence of the three independent Baltic states, Estonia, Latvia and Lithuania. These events created new needs and also new opportunities for both bilateral and multilateral cooperation around the Baltic Sea.

In fact, institutionalized cooperation between the coastal states started back in 1974 with the adoption of the Convention on the Protection of the Marine Environment of the Baltic Sea Area and the establishment of the Helsinki Commission (HelCom) as its governing body. The HelCom contracting parties today are all nine coastal states of the Baltic Sea and the European Union. The Secretariat is in Helsinki, and the chairmanship rotates biennially. Maintaining the marine ecosystems (fish, seals, marine birds), keeping bathing beaches open, combatting toxic algae and other concrete tasks dependent on clean sea water will continue to require sustained efforts for a long time to come.

A new regional organization, the Council of the Baltic Sea States (CBSS), was established on the basis

■ A key objective of Finland's EU policy is to promote the union's "Northern dimension". Much of the Baltic Sea is now surrounded by EU Member States, and the coastal states Poland, Latvia, Lithuania and Estonia have applied for membership. The EU also wishes to support democratization and political stability in Russia and to promote utilization of the country's vast natural resources.

of a Danish-German initiative in 1992. On the highest level, the CBSS is composed of the Ministers for Foreign Affairs from eleven member states, including all five Nordic countries, as well as a member of the European Commission. The Council is intended to encompass all regional inter-governmental cooperation within the group of CBSS countries. The chairmanship rotates on an annual basis, ministerial meetings are held annually, and a committee of senior officials meets more often, while most of the work programme is handled by working groups and task forces. The secretariat of the CBSS is located in Stockholm, and Finland will have the chairmanship again in 2003.

A particularly important aim of the Council of Baltic Sea States has been to consolidate democratic institutions. In this work, the CBSS is assisted by a special working group and by a Commissioner on Democratic Institutions and Human Rights. Economic cooperation with particular emphasis on energy and transport is promoted by another working group as well as by a Baltic Business Advisory Council. The EuroFaculty, located in Riga, assists in reforming higher education at several universities in the region. Environment protection, nuclear safety and combatting organized crime are among the many other fields of action of the CBSS.

Finland is deeply engaged in bilateral cooperation with both the Baltic states and with Russia in a number of specific areas. These activities are mostly funded with Finnish public money in the framework of programmes aiming at the adjacent areas, where Finland has a direct interest. For example, it is obviously important for Finland to assist Russia in the efforts to modernize the sewage treatment plant in the city of St.Petersburg, since the sewage from that city has for a long time contributed to water pollution in

▲ Finland and Estonia are close neighbours and good friends that know each other well. During the summer season, passenger boats make the crossing between the two capitals, Helsinki and Tallinn, about a hundred times daily. The picture shows the Estonian President Arnold Rüütel and the Finnish President Tarja Halonen on the balcony of the presidential palace in Helsinki before talks in November 2001.

the Gulf of Finland. Similarly, Finland has devoted particular attention to assisting its closest neighbour among the Baltic states, Estonia, in strengthening its administration and local government. Finland has also provided equipment and training for members of the Estonian defence forces and border guards. It is clearly in the Finnish interest that Estonia is capable of controlling its own territory effectively.

As for common concerns and challenges in the Arctic region, there are two principal inter-governmental

▲ Protection of the Baltic Sea is an issue of deep concern for all the coastal states. Here, scientists on the Aranda deploy a Seabird CTD sonde, which collects samples of sea water.

organizations with partly overlapping functions: the Arctic Council was established in 1994, and the Barents Euro-Arctic Council (BEAC) in 1993. The former has a circumpolar orientation and counts the five Nordic countries as well as Canada, Russia and the United States as its members. The activities of the BEAC cover only the northern parts of Norway, Sweden, Finland and European Russia, but the European Commission also signed the founding Kirkenes declaration and can be regarded as one of the members. Finland chaired the Arctic Council in 2000–2002 and the BEAC in 1999–2000.

The protection of the vulnerable Arctic environment as well as various cultural and educational programmes, also involving the indigenous peoples of the North and their own organizations, have a central place in the work of both Councils. The BEAC also deals with problems of forestry and natural resources, infrastructure, transport, facilitating border crossings, using the Northern Sea Route and other concrete projects in the region concerned – inhabited by some five million people in an area twice as large as France.

Security policy

In a frequently quoted remark, former President Urho Kekkonen once said that security does not mean erecting a fence but opening a gate. For the security of Finland and its people it is important that Finland has a well-organized, democratic and open society where human rights are respected and the rule of law prevails. It is true that Finland has its share of domestic problems, but there are no extremist movements, nothing that could upset peace and stability. External threats to security in Finland can be perceived in certain long-term trends that affect other countries as well: environmental pollution, climate change, possibly pressures of mass migration. The danger of terrorism cannot be excluded.

There are presently no visible military threats to Finnish security, but in order to meet all contingencies Finland maintains an effective national defence based on universal conscription. All young men are called up for duty, and women are also admitted to serve on a voluntary basis. By maintaining a trained reserve Finland is able to mobilize sizable forces that are capable of defending all parts of the country should the need arise. The ability to control and defend the national territory is in itself a contribution to European security as a whole.

It is also clear that security nowadays is not to be regarded as a purely national matter. Most of the challenges to security require concerted international action. Finland has therefore given strong support to the United Nations, the Organization for Security and Cooperation in Europe and to other international organizations in the security field. This support has also

▲ Between 1956 and 2002, more than 42 000 Finnish soldiers, police and other specialized personnel participated as volunteers in United Nations peacekeeping operations in the Middle East, Cyprus, the Balkans and elsewhere. Finnish soldiers have also served in NATO-led crisis management operations in Bosnia-Herzegovina and Kosovo as well as in coalition operations in Afghanistan. The picture shows Finnish SFOR soldiers in Bosnia-Herzegovina.

◀ The President of Finland, Martti Ahtisaari, meeting journalists in June 1999 in Belgrade, where he had been working out the terms for a settlement over Kosovo on behalf of the European Union together with Victor Chernomyrdin, former Prime Minister of Russia.

taken the form of funds, equipment and personnel contributed to peace-keeping or crisis management operations in several parts of the world.

In the European Union Finland is fully committed to the common foreign and security policy, and Finland has taken an active part in implementing the recent EU decisions aimed at strengthening the defence dimension of the Union. For the time being, this means that the EU is acquiring a military capability that can be used for peace support operations. Whether it will evolve into a full-fledged defence is very uncertain, particularly in view of the general desire to avoid duplication with the work of the North Atlantic Treaty Organization (NATO).

Like other European states, Finland cooperates closely with NATO, both through the partnership programme and via membership in the Euro-Atlantic Partnership Council. Finnish officers have been assigned to various staff posts at NATO headquarters, NATO partnership exercises have been held in Finland, and Finnish troops are currently deployed under NATO leadership in the KFOR and SFOR operations in the Balkans. However, Finland has not applied for membership; the majority of the Finnish people is clearly opposed to the idea of joining NATO, although the government from time to time declares that Finland has an option to join, "if circumstances change". Consequently, the issue of NATO membership remains on the agenda for public debate.

The United Nations system

Finland became a member of the United Nations in 1955, having already joined most of the specialized agencies in the United Nations system much earlier. As a member state, Finland is strongly committed to the goals expressed in the Charter of the United Nations. It is obviously in the interest of Finland to live in a world where international institutions such as the UN bolster the world order and reduce the probability of violence. The actions undertaken by the world organization to promote security and the peaceful settlement of disputes, develop international law, support economic and social development and protect human rights fully match Finland's goals.

In the United Nations, Finland has

EUROPEAN ORGANIZATIONS OF WHICH FINLAND IS A MEMBER
(since year...)

Nordic Council (1955)
Conference on /Organization of Security and Cooperation in Europe CSCE/OSCE (1975)
European Free Trade Association EFTA (1986; associate member 1961)
Council of Europe (1989)
Council of Baltic Sea States CBSS (1992)
North Atlantic Cooperation Council NACC (observer 1992)
Barents Euro-Arctic Council BEAC (1993)
NATO Partnership for Peace PfP (1994)
European Union (1995)
Western European Union WEU (observer 1995)
Arctic Council (1996)
Euro-Atlantic Partnership Council EAPC (successor of NACC, 1997)
Western European Armaments Group WEAG (observer 1997, member 2000)

▶ Finnish women are highly educated. Over half the students in Finnish universities are women. Here, students of Helsinki University.

always worked closely with the other Nordic countries. As a member of the European Union, Finland has had the opportunity since 1995 to take part in shaping the common policies of the EU group in the UN. Other political groupings in which Finland participates, depending on the context, are those of "northern industrialized countries" or "western countries" in general. For electoral purposes, Finland is a member of the Western European and Other Governments Group, which aims to ensure a fair rotation among its members in the available seats on the principal organs of the UN and on various governing bodies and committees. Finland has frequently served as a member of the Economic and Social Council and of the specialized bodies dealing with human rights and development policies. Finland has on two occasions occupied one of the seats in the Security Council: in 1969–1970 and in 1989–1990.

Traditionally, Finland has been one of the principal contributors of military personnel for UN peacekeeping operations. Successful peacekeeping is often carried out by soldiers from small non-aligned countries which are not likely to have interests of their own to pursue in the crisis areas where the UN has been called upon to act. So far, about 40 000 Finnish soldiers have served in twenty different operations as armed peacekeepers, military observers or commanders – in Cyprus, Egypt, Kashmir, Lebanon, Macedonia, Syria and many other parts of the world. In the course of these operations, Finnish soldiers have acquired a solid reputation as reliable and impartial peacekeepers. Finland is one of the Member States that have pledged personnel under the UN stand-by arrangements system, which aims to set up and maintain a rapid deployment capability for future peacekeeping operations.

As a relatively small state without any ambitions of external power projection, Finland has naturally been strongly interested in arms regulation and disarmament. Finland has adhered to all the multilateral conventions in that field that have been prepared in the United Nations. Since 1996, Finland has been a member of the Conference on Disarmament (CD) in Geneva. The task of the Conference is to draft new treaties for consideration by the General Assembly. For many years before becoming a member, Finland worked closely with the CD, in particular in the study and elaboration of systems for verifying chemical disarmament.

In the area of human rights, Finland has adhered to all the major covenants and conventions as well as to the optional arrangements that make it possible to institute international complaints procedures in cases of alleged violations of human rights. One of

Finland's priorities has been action for gender equality, where Finnish experience may offer opportunities for input into United Nations programmes. In order to contribute to the suppression of crimes against humanity, Finland has been a staunch supporter of the International Criminal Court that started functioning in 2002.

As regards the administration and financing of the world organization, Finland has consistently emphasized the duty of all Member States to pay their obligatory contributions to the UN in full and on time. With the other Nordic countries, Finland has in recent years made a point of paying its membership dues for each beginning year right after the New Year holiday, thus hoping to relieve the UN Secretariat of some of the persistent financial difficulties caused by arrears in the inflow of contributions. The administrative reforms carried out over recent years under the leadership of Secretary-General Kofi Annan have received the full support of the Finnish government.

Relations with the United States

Historically, Finland has always had good relations with the United States of America. Finns accounted for a large share of the contingent of settlers sent from Sweden to the North American continent in the 17th century. Like many other European countries, Finland later shared in the mass movement of emigrants to North America at the end of the 19th century and in the years that followed. Altogether some 320 000 emigrants from Finland have settled in the United States. Consequently, there are large communities of Americans of Finnish origin, particularly in Michigan, Minnesota and Wisconsin. The descendants of Finns who arrived seeking jobs and higher living standards a hundred years ago have maintained contact with the land of their forefathers, thus ensuring strong personal bonds between Finland and the United States. Annual "Finnfest" gatherings bring together Finnish-

▼ About 320 000 Finns have emigrated to America. The largest group of emigrants left in the late 19th and early 20th century. The picture shows a family of Finnish settlers in front of their newly completed, modest first home.

Americans in the United States, and there are still newspapers, associations, cooperatives, colleges and other institutions serving the Finnish-American communities, although assimilation in the great American melting pot has of course reduced their significance over the years. If all persons of Finnish origin are counted down to the fourth generation, there were at the end of the 20th century some 700 000 expatriate Finns living in the United States.

During the years of the depression in the 1930's, Finland acquired the reputation of being "the country that pays its debts"; as other countries defaulted, Finland continued its payments even during the second World War. On the initiative of Senator William Fulbright, the remaining payments were in 1949 converted into a fund for sending Finnish graduate students to study and do research in the United States. The original loans have been paid, but the programmes for educational exchange between Finland and the United States continue to this day in a broadened and diversified form. Every year a total of more than one hundred academic teachers and graduate students from the two countries spend productive periods of study and research in the United States and in Finland.

Throughout the years of the cold war Finland made a point of maintaining its traditionally good relations with the United States. Finland declined to take part in the Marshall plan, but benefited from other American credits granted in the post-war period to support reconstruction and recovery. In the shadow of the Soviet Union, struggling to uphold a posture of neutrality between the main protagonists of the cold war, the friendship with the United States played an important political and psychological role. The engagement of the United States in Europe as a political and military counter-balance to the Soviet Union was important for the stability of the continent as a whole.

▲ **President George Bush and Mrs. Barbara Bush visited Helsinki in 1990. They were met at Helsinki-Vantaa airport by President Mauno Koivisto and Mrs. Tellervo Koivisto.**

This stability was of crucial significance not only for the allies of the United States but also for countries like Finland.

Today, the ties of Finland to the United States are as strong as ever. Many of the economic and political relations have of course been handled through the European Union since Finland became a member in 1995, but direct contacts are also important. The United States is Finland's third trade partner overall. Finland imports civilian and military aircraft, computers, motor vehicles and other products of high technology, but American consumer goods also find their way to the Finnish market.

Emigration to Australia and Canada

Historically Finland has been a country of net emigration. Of the close to half a million persons who moved out of Finland before the second World War, the United States attracted the largest number, but Canada was the second most favoured country of destination and received some 70 000 Finnish emigrants. In the period after the second World War, Canada was the major non-European recipient of Finnish emigrants until about 1960, when Australia took the leading place. All in all, Canada has over the years since the late 19th century received some 87 000 emigrants from Finland, and Australia has received more than 20 000. In Canada, the Finnish settlers are concentrated mostly in the province of Ontario, but there are also sizable communities in British Columbia and Alberta. The ties to Australia are inevitably affected by the long physical distance between the two countries, but Finland benefits for example from the fruitful partnership in science and technology that has been developed between the European Union and Australia.

Cooperation with countries of Africa, Asia and Latin America

Apart from the exploits of a few adventurous travellers and the patient efforts of missionaries, Finns have traditionally had only few direct contacts with the large continents of Africa, Asia and Latin America. In the absence of historical ties to those parts of the world, trade has opened the way. Finland is highly dependent on international trade, and nowadays Finnish business corporations also seek partnerships and opportunities for investment everywhere. Countries of rapid growth like China and some of the South-East Asian countries play a significant role in Finland's foreign economic rela-

▶ For obvious reasons, Finland has no history as a colonial nation, although there were some Finns among the Swedish settlers of Delaware in North America in the 17th century. The earliest contacts with Africa were established by missionaries. Dr. Selma Rainio (1873–1939) was one of the pioneering women missionaries. After completing her medical studies at the University of Helsinki, she left for Ovamboland in Namibia in 1908 to work as a missionary physician. She introduced training for hospital nurses in the country and opened the way for women who had previously been assigned to menial tasks in fields dominated by male personnel.

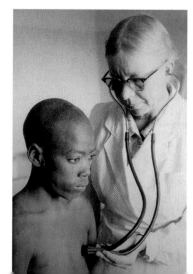

▶ Mozambique is now Finland's main partner for development co-operation in Africa. Funds have been allocated to forestry development, basic education and the meteorological service. Here Suvi-Anne Siimes, Minister for Development Cooperation, visits the weather service of the Mozambique Meteorological Institute (INAM) in Maputo. Finland and EU are funding the upgrading of weather services and the development of an early warning system for natural disasters.

tions. The total share of Africa, Asia and Latin America in Finland's foreign trade is about 16%.

Furthermore, since the middle of the twentieth century, awareness of the global problems related to unbalanced economic development has played an important part in public discourse. In creating and implementing its own programmes of cooperation for development, Finland has gone through several stages. Early on, Finland adopted a few regions or countries as partners for bilateral assistance efforts

▶ Telecommunications are a boom industry in China. The number of mobile phones has soared in recent years: by February 2002, there were 156 million subscribers. Nokia mobile phones on show at a telecommunications fair in Beijing.

(such as Kerala in India and Tanzania in Africa). At the same time Finland contributed to several multilateral development programmes, mainly under the auspices of the United Nations system.

Gradually Finnish development efforts became more sophisticated, and more funds were made available in the Finnish state budget. Most of the Finnish activities are administered by the Department for Development Cooperation in the Finnish Ministry for Foreign Affairs (FINNIDA). Political parties and many non-governmental organizations continue to play an active part in debating development policies and advancing their own ideas and priorities.

North-South questions occupy a prominent place in the United Nations system, and Finland has been an active member of many specialized bodies working in that field, seeking not only to reduce the quantitative gap in living standards between developing and industrialized countries, but also to promote environment protection and human rights. The quantitative and qualitative aspects of Finnish development policies are regularly examined by the Development Assistance Committee (DAC) of the OECD, which has 21 members.

The UN General Assembly has set the figure of 0.7% of the gross national product as the target for net transfers of assistance from industrialized countries. Finland has accepted this goal, and even reached it in the year 1991, when Finnish development contributions reached 0.80% of GNP. During the recession of the early 1990s, the figure went down again, and in recent years it has remained close to the EU average at about 0.34%. The government's current goal is to raise the level of assistance slowly, in order to reach 0.4% by 2007 or 2008.

About one third of Finnish development assistance is channelled to various forms of multilateral assistance, one third goes to bilateral development cooperation, and the remaining third is reserved for refugees, humanitarian assistance, and support to non-governmental organizations and other causes.

Working in cooperation with the UN High Commissioner for Refugees, Finland has received refugees from countries like Chile, Somalia, Vietnam, and Yugoslavia as well as from the Kurdish areas in Iran, Iraq and Turkey. The refugee population in Finland is still fairly small compared with other European countries: of some 150 000 inhabitants born outside the country, fewer than 20 000 are refugees.

A Land
of Many Faces

Finland is a place with a character all its own, where East and West merge. The history, culture and religion of the country set the Finns squarely among the peoples of Western Europe; and yet the eastern influence is strong. A similar contrast characterizes the Finnish landscape. Southern Finland features groves of deciduous trees such as oak, while the central region is dotted with lakes and conifer forests, and the north is a land of bare fells, open expanses and dwarf birch.

A varied landscape

A sparsely populated country in the far northeastern corner of Europe, Finland is nevertheless a mid-sized European state in terms of land area. Almost one quarter of the country's territory lies north of the Arctic Circle, making Finland the world's northernmost country together with Iceland. In the south and west, Finland is bounded by the Baltic Sea, offering a direct sea route to the Continent. The broken coastline in the southwest gradually gives way to the Saaristomeri, or Archipelago Sea, unique in the world for the multitude, variety and closeness of its islands. All in all, Finland's territorial waters count over 80,000 islands, the two largest being the main island of the Åland group and Kemiö, just southeast of Turku.

Finland lies on the western fringe of the Eurasian boreal coniferous zone, the *taiga*. The forests are characterized by a paucity of species: the only trees of any economic significance are pine, spruce, birch and, to a lesser extent,

alder and aspen. Although Finland extends from the northern boundary of the oak zone to the bare subarctic fells, the country has no mountain ranges proper. The highest altitudes are in the country's northwestern "arm", the Enontekiö region, an outlier of the Scandic fells featuring Finland's highest peak Haltiatunturi (or Halti, 1328 metres).

The lie of the land is characterized by small-scale variation. Most of the country is low-lying, and slopes gently towards the south or southeast. Eastern Finland is dotted with lakes and high hills; the rolling landscape of Central Finland gives way in the west to the Ostrobothnian plains, with hillocks and lowlands in other coastal areas. The bare, rugged fells of Lapland are separated by canyons gouged by turbulent rivers.

The topography is founded on the

▶ The Finnish landscape is dotted with lakes, islands and forests.

ancient bedrock, most of which was formed some 1 800–1 900 million years ago. In contrast, the soil is very young, for the glaciers of the last Ice Age carried off virtually all loose matter. A reminder of this relatively recent period of glaciation is the uplift phenomenon, which continues to remodel the landscape, increasing the country's land area by some 7 square kilometres every year.

Finland has something like 188,000 lakes, more than almost any other country in the world. Lakes constitute about 10 per cent of Finland's total area; indeed, in some parts of the country a quarter or even half of the surface is under water. Most of the lakes are very small, but the largest, Greater Saimaa, ranks fourth in Europe and forty-third in the world.

The rivers are mostly short and have a relatively small discharge, as none of the watersheds are far from the coast. The principal watershed is called Maanselkä, which separates the rivers running into the Baltic Sea (91%) from those discharging into the Arctic Ocean and the White Sea. The longest river is Kemijoki-Kitinen (552 km).

The aquatic environment is unique. The smooth-worn bedrock, the Ice Age and uplift have together created a veritable maze of waterways. The large lakes of central Finland are virtually at the same altitude. Between them meanders an endless succession of narrows and slow-flowing straits, interspersed with inlets, headlands and islands. The lakes contain a total of nearly 100,000 islands, the second highest number in the world after Canada.

◄ Finland's four seasons.

Some 70% of the land area is productive forest, making Finland the most densely forested country in Europe. The proportion of mires is higher than anywhere else in the world. If poor-growth forest is included, wetlands represent almost one third of Finland's territory.

Finland's fauna is similar to that of Scandinavia and northern Russia, consisting mostly of species typical of the boreal coniferous zone, such as the brown bear, the national animal. In addition, arctic species are found in the north and typical European species in the south. The fauna have arrived so recently that few species are endemic, a rare exception being the ringed seal of Saimaa, a protected species that is a relict from the post-glacial era.

► During the last glacial epoch, the ringed seal was cut off from the sea and stranded in the Lake Saimaa water system. It is an endangered species today, its survival threatened mainly by motorboats and fishermen's nets, in which the seals often become entangled.

In February 1996, the biggest snow castle in the world was inaugurated in the town of Kemi in northern Finland. It featured over 400 metres of walls and an auditorium with seating for 1 500 spectators. More than 270 000 people came to see it that winter, and the town decided to build a new castle every year to attract winter tourists and to serve as a cultural centre. The people have kept coming, and in 2001 the castle had 110 000 visitors. The secret to the castle's success is its uniqueness and potential for innovation. Since the castle has to be built from scratch every year,

there is plenty of scope for technical experimentation, while the builders learn from past years' experience.

West wind, polar night and midnight sun

The Finnish climate is a great deal milder than might be expected given the northern location of the country. The cold is moderated by the Baltic Sea, the inland waters and, above all, the westerly winds bringing in Atlantic air warmed by the Gulf Stream. The mean temperature in Finland is between 6°C and 10°C higher than elsewhere in the world at similar latitudes.

The winters are relatively humid and cold. The occasional continental fronts that push in from the east cause severe frosts in the winter and heat waves in the summer. During the coldest winters the temperature in the north may fall to −40°C or even −50°C, whereas readings of up to +35°C have been recorded during the brief summer. Many visitors find the sharp sea-

▲ ▼ For centuries, travellers have been drawn to Lapland to marvel at the midnight sun. More recent innovations are polar night tours and visits to Father Christmas' home region. Above, the midnight sun stains the whole sky a yellowish red. Below, the moon provides the only relief to the gloom of the polar night.

sonal shifts hard to get used to.

Winter is the longest season in Finland. In northernmost Lapland, the polar night, or *kaamos*, lasts 52 days, while the southern parts of the country have just six hours of daylight in the darkest midwinter period. The light of summer makes up for the winter darkness. On the south coast, the sun is up for almost 19 hours at midsummer. In Nuorgam in the far north, the sun does not set for 67 days. Although rain or snow falls throughout the year, overall precipitation is not evenly divided. The early summer tends to be too dry for the farmers' liking, especially in the southwest and along the Ostrobothnian coast, whereas rainfall is often excessive at the end of the growing season (the period during which the average daily temperature exceeds 5°C). This season lasts about two months longer in the south than in the north, although the difference is offset somewhat by the fact that Lapland's mid-night sun provides plants with a larger daily dose of light during the summer.

Natural resources and the environment

Finland has a wealth of natural resources in terms of both raw materials and sources of energy. Most of these – including the most important resource, wood – are renewable. Finland's overall forest reserves (1930 million cubic metres) are Europe's fourth largest after Russia, Sweden and Germany. Annual forest growth amounts to almost 75 million cubic metres. Another major resource is water, which is used by both households and industry, and as a source of energy.

PUBLIC RIGHT OF ACCESS IN FINLAND

■ Public right of access (the Finnish term *jokamiehenoikeus* means "everyman's right") means that every citizen has access to the land, regardless of who owns it. You don't have to ask the owner for permission to enter his land, and normally don't have to pay a fee either. Naturally you mustn't damage the owner's property or disturb his peace. On the Finnish mainland, this right comprises:
– the right of access on foot, on skis, or by bicycle; off limits are courtyards, fields, meadows and planted areas susceptible to damage; camping at a reasonable distance from habitation is permitted;
– the right to pick wild berries, mushrooms and flowers, as long as they are not protected species;

– the right of access to water for boating, bathing and washing; the right to travel over ice.

The rules in the Åland Islands differ from those on the mainland on a few points: certain rights available to everyone on the mainland are restricted in Åland to permanent residents.

▶ National parks have been established for the protection of various biotopes, including peat-land, waters, fells and forests. Oulankajoki National Park near Kuusamo is a paradise for hikers, especially when the autumn colours are at their height.

◀ ▼ The swan and the bear are national symbols.

Non-renewable resources derive from inorganic nature. Finland's bedrock contains many rock types suitable for use as industrial raw material. Ore resources are also varied; even some promising diamond and gold deposits have been discovered in recent years. The most valuable non-renewable resources are gravel, sand, clay and peat (classified as non-renewable because it takes so long to form).

The environment is exceptionally intact and unpolluted. Nevertheless, the Finns have been paying increasing attention to conservation in the last few years. The most important sector of environmental protection is water conservation. Most of the pollutants released into the environment eventually wind up in the waters. In Finland these are shallow and thus easily contaminated. Half of the overall air pollution is caused by indigenous sources, while the other half consists of transboundary pollution.

There is a wide variety of nature conservation areas, and the most important are classified as nature reserves or national parks. Visitors need a special permit to enter one of the 19 nature reserves. The 33 national parks serve the purposes of research, education and recreation. There are also special conservation areas for wetlands, deciduous groves, shores and old-growth forests. The Natura 2000 conservation programme was enacted in 1998 in accordance with the EU environmental directives. Under the programme, 12 per cent of Finland's area is protected.

Population

The Finns' forefathers first came to the shores of Finland some time between 9000 and 8000 B.C. They found a barren coastline, laid waste by the retreating continental ice shelf. The settlers arrived from at least two different directions, east and south. Finland has remained settled ever since that time. Over the centuries, new waves of settlers arrived from different directions, but they were all assimilated into the earlier population.

Extremely sparsely settled for many centuries, Finland has seen a prolonged period of population growth in the 20th

NATIONAL CHARACTER

■ Zachris Topelius (1818–1898) was the best-known portrayer of his country and its people, and has had perhaps a stronger influence than anyone else on the way the Finns perceive themselves. According to Topelius, the Finnish national character could be summed up in four words: cautious, stubborn, taciturn and imperturbable. All these qualities stem directly from Finland's stark nature.

Blond hair and blue eyes are often thought of as typically Finnish features. According to a rough estimate, three quarters of the Finns' genetic makeup is of Baltic-Germanic origin and one quarter of Eastern origin.

century. The population first surpassed three million in 1914 and attained four million in 1950. As a result of the postwar baby boom, the population reached four and a half million by 1965. Around this time, the birth rate sagged, and what with mass emigration to Sweden in search of jobs, the population actually decreased in 1969 and 1970.

Population growth picked up somewhat in the 1980s, as many emigrants returned and the birth rate increased. The five-million mark was reached in 1991, and by January 2002 Finland had a population of 5,190,000. Demographically, the country is characterized by a high proportion of working-age people and a steadily aging population. Children (0 to 14) account for less than one fifth of the population, while the proportion of senior citizens (over 65s) is 15%. Over two thirds of the Finns are in the working-age category (15 to 64).

Over 51% of the country's population are women. This is primarily due to a higher mortality rate among men; more boys are born than girls. Women account for more than two thirds of the senior citizens category. The population is unusually homogeneous, as the only indigenous ethnic minorities are the Sámi and the Romany. The majority of the 4,500 Sámi live in the Sámi home region in the northernmost municipalities of Lapland, while the 6,000-strong Romany population are more evenly distributed throughout the country.

The proportion of foreigners is among the lowest in Europe. At the end of 2000, just over 91,000 foreign citizens were living in Finland. The number of immigrants from the former Soviet Union, however, has grown rapidly in recent years. Between 1973 and 2000, refugees arrived primarily from Asia (e.g. Vietnam), Somalia and the former Yugoslavia.

▼ Finland has two official languages, Finnish and Swedish. In bilingual communities, street names and road signs are in both languages.

The official languages are Finnish and Swedish; Sámi has official status within the Sámi home region. Finnish, a language belonging to the Finno-Ugric family, holds an uncontested dominant position, being spoken by almost 93% of the population. Fewer than 6% of the Finns speak Swedish as their mother tongue; most of them live on the south or west coast or in the Åland Islands.

Finnish is a very distinctive language and the only non-Indo-European language of the European Union. Perhaps because of this "different" quality of the language, no satisfactory translation has ever been produced of the greatest and most Finnish of all Finnish novels, Aleksis Kivi's nineteenth-century masterpiece *The Seven Brothers*. Few people outside the country's borders speak Finnish, but the language can be studied at more than 90 universities abroad today.

Irregular settlement

Finland is Europe's third most sparsely populated country after Iceland and Norway. The population density at the beginning of 2002 was 17 persons per square kilometre. Although the country is settled throughout, the population density varies greatly. The principal city and capital is Helsinki, which had about 560,000 inhabitants in 2002. Nearly 970,000 people lived in the Helsinki Metropolitan Area, which includes the neighbouring agglomerations of Espoo, Vantaa and Kauniainen. This functionally coherent capital region can be compared with the similar regions of Stockholm, Oslo and Copenhagen.

The third largest city after Helsinki and Espoo is Tampere, the largest inland settlement in the Nordic coun-

tries. Turku, Finland's capital until 1812, is currently the fifth largest city (Vantaa being no. 4).

▲ Helsinki is known as the White City of the North. Here, the city centre as seen from the sea. The Swedish Embassy in the centre, with the Cathedral dome soaring high above it. In the foreground Kauppatori, the main market.

Rising housing standards

Housing is an even more vital requirement in the north than in milder climates. The Finn's life centres on the home and its immediate surroundings. Much of the housing stock was replaced during the construction boom of the 1970s and '80s, while in the 1990s the focus shifted to renovation and refurbishment.

Most Finns would prefer to live in a house of their own, surrounded by a private garden. Large-scale construction of single-family houses, however, only really got under way in the late 1970s. Today there are almost as many single-family homes as flats: both account for over 40% of total housing. The proportion of other low-rise housing, such as terraced houses and rowhouses, is also on the rise.

Urbanization came late to Finland, and a large part of the population still long for the peace and quiet of the country. Many are therefore willing to make do with a cramped apartment in the city to be able to afford a summer cottage of their own. There are over 450,000 such second homes in Finland, most of them on the coast or by a lakeside.

Another obligatory feature of Finnish housing is the sauna bath, of which there are 1.3 million in the country. The sauna is sacred to the Finns; its significance might be compared with that of the tea ceremony to the Japanese. Every block of flats, even every individual house – not to speak of summer cottages – must have its own sauna. Bathing in a sauna has an incomparable cleansing and relaxing effect, especially when accompanied by a dip in cool water. In the winter, the hardiest bathers sometimes roll in the snow to cool off.

Tourism

Finland is too far north to ever become a target for mass tourism. Its main attractions are a safe, stable social fabric, sparse settlement and untouched nature. Whereas in most countries landowners may prevent or restrict entry

▲ Life without a sauna, a sanctuary for physical and mental relaxation, would be unthinkable for the Finns. The best saunas are built on the waterfront.

to their land with fences and notices, in Finland there are few restrictions to access: you are free to wander at will and gather native berries, mushrooms and flowers even on private land.

Finland provides a rich range of culture, nature and adventure tourism. Myriad summer music events offer the finest international quality in authentic Finnish settings, the three most famous being the Savonlinna Opera Festival, the Kuhmo Chamber Music Festival and the Pori Jazz Festival. Vast forests and winding waterways provide excellent opportunities for adventure

▲ Snowmobile and husky safaris are among Lapland's biggest tourist attractions.

NORTHERN LIGHTS

■ The Northern lights (or aurora borealis) are an optical phenomenon occurring most frequently near the magnetic poles. They arise when electrically charged particles powered by the solar wind and travelling at great speed collide with atoms and molecules in the atmosphere. The collision excites these atoms and molecules, which emit a photon as they discharge.

The usual colour of the Northern lights is yellowish green, emitted by oxygen atoms generally some 90 to 150 kilometres above the earth's surface. The red aurora occasionally sighted above the green also stems from oxygen atoms, while ionized nitrogen molecules emit blue and purple light. The aurora borealis occurs in both summer and winter, but in the summer it never gets dark enough for the lights to be visible. In Finland you are likeliest to get a glimpse of the aurora on a late winter evening in northern Lapland, but from time to time they shine brightly in the southern parts of the country, too.

The main centre for research on the Northern lights is in Sodankylä.

▲ As almost everyone knows, Father Christmas lives in Finland, setting out in Rudolph the Red-Nosed Reindeer's sleigh to distribute presents to all the world's children.

Finland's reputation as a winter holiday destination has grown steadily. The main attractions are cross-country and Alpine skiing, snowboarding, snowmobile safaris and husky-drawn sleighrides. The popularity of many winter resorts is enhanced by spas of high standard; indeed, Finland is the leading Nordic country in terms of the number of bathing resorts. The largest numbers of visitors come from Sweden and Russia; the Germans are the third biggest tourist group in Finland.

In dark December, tourists are drawn to Finland by the one and only genuine Father Christmas. Tens of thousands of visitors, great and small, travel from Britain alone to see him. With the rapid increase in his popularity, Father Christmas has continually enlarged his domain. Santapark, an underground amusement park near the Santa Claus Workshop Village on the Arctic Circle, opened at the end of 1998.

Finland is also a popular congress country, not least because many meetings between the world's leaders here have shown that the Finns are capable organizers of safe, smoothly functioning, high-profile international events. Almost 300 international conferences are held in the country every year, attracting a total of over 55,000 participants, many of whom travel with a companion. Excellent transport connections ensure that a conference in Finland can easily be combined with a holiday in some other part of the country or in Russia or one of the Baltic countries. The car ferries operating between Sweden and Finland are real "floating hotels" and a major attraction in their own right.

tourism, often arranged by companies for their staff, and give hikers, canoeists and fishing enthusiasts inexhaustible opportunities to explore and test their survival skills. Thousands of well-fitted holiday homes provide the perfect opportunity for relaxation and privacy far from the city crowds. Finland's over 60 full-size golf courses offer visitors the magic of natural light around the clock in summer.

Finland through the Centuries

The continental ice sheet that covered Finland began to retreat some 10,000 years ago. The thick ice cover had pressed down on the earth's crust with such force that the land was mostly under water. The land soon began to rise, however, and people started arriving from two directions: the east and the south. The earliest signs of human habitation in Finland date from 8000–7000 B.C.

During the Stone Age (7000–1400 B.C.), settlements were established near water. The early settlers were hunters and fishermen; animal husbandry and farming were introduced by new settlers around 2500 B.C. During the Bronze Age (c. 1400 B.C.– 500 B.C..) the cultural differences between inland dwellers and the coastal population deepened, as the coastal areas were increasingly influenced by the west and the inland areas by the east.

The beginning of the Iron Age has been dated to 500 B.C. According to earlier scholars, the forefathers of the present-day Finns crossed the Gulf of Finland at or just after the beginning of the Christian Era. More recent scholarship, however, tends to the view that although Iron Age civilization was enriched by new impulses from the south, there was never any "great migration" to Finland. The Finns, in fact, never "came from" somewhere else; their ancestors peopled the land without interruption since the Stone Age, and the Finnish language and identity formed here over the centuries. During the Viking era (c. 800–1050 A.D.), also known as the final years of the "pre-historic" period, contacts with the world outside increased as a result of Finland's position along the Vikings' eastern trade route, and trading outposts were established along the coast. From these, settlers moved inland and the population density increased. Some Finns probably took part in the Viking voyages.

Finland in the kingdom of Sweden

Until the twelfth century, Finland was a religious and political hinterland, coveted by its western neighbour Sweden and the Catholic Church on the one hand, and by its eastern neighbour the Principality of Novgorod (later Russia) and the Orthodox Church on the other. In 1155 or thereabouts the Swedes made a military expedition, later known as the First Crusade, to the southwest coast of Finland, which gave them a base for spreading the Christian religion and consolidating their secular power. In 1238 the Swedes strengthened their hold on Finland with the Second Crusade, taking them far inland into the region of Häme.

The eastern border is drawn

With the Swedes tightening their grip on western Finland, Novgorod pushed in from the east to the region of Karelia. Alarmed by this development, Sweden embarked on its Third Crusade in 1293, reaching the mouth of the Gulf of Finland and building a fortress at Viipuri (Wiborg). Thus Sweden had won the race for the conquest of Finland. The Treaty of Pähkinäsaari (Schlüsselburg, today Petrokrepost) established the border between Sweden and Novgorod, leaving only the eastern part of Karelia to the latter.

Thus western and southern Finland came within the sphere of influence of West European culture, whereas the Russo-Byzantine culture left its imprint on the eastern parts of the country. The annexed Finnish provinces became known in Sweden as "the Eastland," a name first recorded in the

1340s. The principal town of this region and the bishop's see was Turku, founded in the mid thirteenth century.

As part of Sweden, the Finns had some say in the affairs of the nation. In 1362, they were granted the right to take part in the election of the king, and they also sent representatives to the Diet of Estates. At the end of the Middle Ages (in the early years of the sixteenth century), Finland had a population of some 350,000. Most of these were small farmers; even the largest towns were still of very modest size.

Gustavus Vasa ascended to the Swedish throne in 1523. He pursued a dual policy of increasing both the power and the revenues of the Crown. The Reformation, started just before this in Germany by Martin Luther, suited the royal plans perfectly, and so the Church of Rome rapidly lost its position to Lutheranism. The Reformation marked the beginning of the cultural role of vernacular languages. Mikael Agricola, Bishop of Turku and the father of written Finnish, translated numerous works into the vernacular, including the New Testament (1548). The full text of the Bible was first published in Finnish almost a century later, in 1642.

▼ **King Erik of Sweden set off on his first crusade to Finland with the Scottish-born Bishop Henry around 1155. Henry stayed behind in Finland to convert and baptize the pagan Finns. According to legend, the farmer Lalli attacked and killed Henry on the ice of a frozen lake. The picture shows St. Henry surrounded by holy men, with his murderer prostrate at his feet.**

▲ Construction of Turku Castle began in the late thirteenth century and continued for many centuries. The castle's heyday came during the Renaissance in the 1560s, when Duke John and his spouse Catharine Iagellonica held court there.

▼ King Gustav Vasa of Sweden confiscated the property of the Catholic Church throughout the country and ordered his subjects to convert to Lutheranism. This sketch by Albert Edelfelt shows Mikael Agricola, who studied under the tuition of Martin Luther and eventually became Bishop of Finland, presenting his Finnish translation of the New Testament to the king.

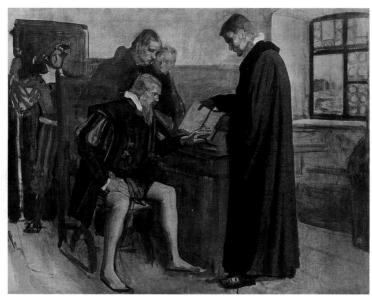

Splendour and misery of a great power

In the seventeenth century, Sweden expanded its territory around the whole Baltic Sea, pushing the eastern border of Finland further east as a result. Sweden's heyday was a time of wholesale progress in Finland, but it also meant increasingly centralized rule, as Stockholm tightened its administrative grip on the provinces. As it expanded, Sweden was obliged to strain its forces to the utmost. For its constant wars, the mother country conscripted an endless stream of Finnish soldiers. The province's misery was compounded by the famine of 1696 and 1697, when hunger and disease killed nearly one third of Finland's population.

Sweden's position as a great power came to an end with the disastrous war of 1700–1721, known as the Great Northern War. The Russians occupied Finland during this war, but in the Treaty of Uusikaupunki (Nystad) in 1721 all the Finnish provinces except for the southeastern part of the country reverted to Sweden. Despite intermittent wars with Russia after this, the eighteenth century brought Finland an increase in population and economic improvement. Indeed, the population soared from 306,000 in the 1720s to 907,000 in 1807.

Industrialization got off to a cautious start with the founding of a handful of factories, including a glassworks, a sugar refinery and a paper mill. The most important industry at the time, however, was the production of sawn goods. Finland exported planks, tar and ships, and imported grain and salt as well as luxuries such as tobacco and coffee.

The first Finnish-language newspaper was founded in 1776. Many a leading scholar taught at the Academy of Turku, which had been founded back in 1640. Pehr Kalm, professor of economics, became famous for his journey to North America; Johan Gadolin, professor of chemistry, discovered a new group of elements, and Henrik Gabriel Porthan, professor of Latin and polymath, was the first to study Finnish language, history and poetry.

▼ Finland's first university, The Academy of Turku was founded in 1640.

▲ Tsar Alexander I opened the first Diet of Finland in 1809, raising Finland "to the rank of nations". Painting by Emanuel Thelning.

▼ Tsar Nicholas II appointed Nikolai Bobrikov Governor-General of Finland in 1898 and charged him with the task of "Russifying" the province. The February Manifesto aimed at suppressing Finland's right to its own laws. Almost 530 000 Finns signed an appeal to the Tsar, and 1050 European scientists and scholars signed "the European Address Pro Finlandia". The Tsar did not acknowledge either address. Shown here is the highly decorated first page of the Swedish address.

▼ "Deep matters" (knowledge and wisdom) are treated in the Kalevala, the Finnish national epic.

▲ It was largely Johan Vilhelm Snellman's doing that the Grand Duchy of Finland was granted its own currency, the *markka,* in 1860. This marked a major step on the road to full independence from Russia.

Grand Duchy of the Russian Empire

A new leaf in Finnish history was turned in winter 1808, as Russia declared war on Sweden and invaded Finland. The War of Finland, as this conflict is known, ended in Sweden's defeat, and in the peace treaty of 1809 Sweden ceded Finland to Russia. Thus almost seven centuries of Swedish rule in Finland had come to an end.

Russia awarded its newly-annexed province the status of a grand duchy. The Tsar of Russia was thus also Grand Duke of Finland, and his representative in the country was the Governor-General. The laws enacted during the Swedish period remained in force, and the Lutheran Church retained its leading position. The grand duchy was endowed with an administration of its own, with Swedish as the language of government. This extensive autonomy made Finland a unique entity of the Russian Empire, in effect a state within a state. The supreme executive body was the Senate (a kind of Government), whose members were all Finns. The Senate submitted decisions directly to the Tsar, past the Russian ministers and civil service.

The Russians did not think Turku a suitable capital for the grand duchy, as it was both culturally and geographically too close to Sweden. Helsinki was therefore made the capital of Finland by imperial decree in 1812.

Period of reform

Alexander I died in 1825 and was succeeded by Nicholas I. Although a reactionary ruler, the "Soldier Tsar" upheld Finland's autonomy. It was in fact under his rule that the nationalist Finnish movement began to gain momentum. The *Kalevala*, compiled by Elias Lönnrot and soon hailed as the Finnish national epic, was published in 1835; J.L. Runeberg, "the national poet" (who wrote in Swedish), produced a series of patriotic ballads.

J.V. Snellman, philosopher and senator, demanded that Finnish should replace Swedish as the language of the civil service and the educated class. The liberal Alexander II, who became Tsar in 1855, issued the "Language Manifesto" in 1863, according to which Finnish should be accorded equal status with Swedish as a language of the civil service and courts of law within twenty years. Nonetheless, Swedish retained its dominant position until the early years of the twentieth century.

Alexander I had convened the first Finnish Diet in 1809, but the Diet did not meet again until 1863. From that time, however, it was convened regularly, resulting in a whole spate of new legislation. The country's local government was overhauled, an elementary school system was introduced, and the 1878 Act on National Service founded a separate Finnish Army. Finland had already been given its own currency, the mark (*markka* in Finnish), in 1860.

Russification

The rise of Nicholas II to the throne in 1894 meant an increase in the influence of Russian ultranationalists. The Grand Duchy of Finland was a part of the Empire, to be sure, but sheltered by extensive privileges, and thus

▶ Marshal C. G. E. Mannerheim inspects the troops during military exercises in the Karelian Isthmus, 1939. Mannerheim served as regent after the Finnish Civil War from December 1918 until K.J. Ståhlberg was sworn in as Finland's first president in the summer of 1919. Marshal Mannerheim served as commander-in-chief of the Finnish army during the Winter War and Continuation War and then as President of Finland from 1944 to 1946.

a thorn in their flesh. The eradication of what they saw as Finnish separatism began during the "First Russification" from 1899 to 1905, and continued during the "Second Russification" from 1909 to 1917.

The Revolution of 1905 gave the Finns a brief respite, during which they managed to enact a new Constitution replacing the old Diet of Four Estates with a unicameral Parliament elected by universal suffrage applying to all men and women aged 24 or more. This was the most democratic national assembly in Europe at the time.

The Independent Republic

The First World War, which broke out in summer 1914, led to revolution in Russia in 1917. The February Revolution resulted in the deposition

of the Tsar, and the October Revolution brought the Bolsheviks to power. Breaking with the revolutionary regime, the Finnish Parliament, in which the non-socialist parties had the majority, proclaimed itself the supreme authority in Finland on November 15. With its newly- assumed powers, Parliament appointed a new Senate (Government) under P.E. Svinhufvud. Finland proclaimed itself independent on the basis of the Senate's proposal on December 6, 1917.

In the wake of the Bolshevik uprising in Russia, the gap between right and left also widened in Finland, soon reaching unbridgeable proportions. The situation was aggravated by the continued presence of some 70,000 Russian soldiers in Finland in early 1918. At the end of January, the extreme left and the Red Guard rebelled, and the Senate was forced to flee Helsinki. In the ensuing civil war, the Senate received assistance from Germany, while the rebels were aided by Soviet Russia. The war ended in mid-May 1918 in victory for the Senate troops under General C.G.E. Mannerheim.

Building the Republic

At the close of the civil war, the plan was to make Finland a monarchy with a German king, but following the collapse of Germany in November 1918, Finland had to shift its political allegiance westwards, and adopted a republican form of government. K.J. Ståhlberg was elected first President of the Republic in summer 1919.

Construction of the new independent republic now got under way. A law on compulsory education was enacted in 1921, and compulsory military service the next year. A language controversy between speakers of Finnish and Swedish festered throughout the 1920s. The unpopular Prohibition Act, enacted in 1919, was repealed in 1932.

▲ The Winter War lasted three and a half months, during which Finland repelled the massive attacks of the Soviet Union time after time. During this exceptionally cold winter, the Soviets learned to fear the Finnish ski patrols, which were likely to turn up without a sound where they were least expected.

▼ The Lotta organization (women's auxiliary corps) provided invaluable services during the war. Its members provisioned and nursed troops even at the front. This photo from the Continuation War shows a nurse giving wounded soldiers water.

The left-wing parties got a taste of power as the country had its first Social Democratic government from 1926 to 1927. The ultra-rightist Lapua Movement, modelled on the Italian Fascist party, staged mass demonstrations in 1929, demanding a ban on all Communist activity. The enactment of the "Communist laws" of 1930 met this demand. The final effort of the Lapuaists came with an uprising in 1932, but this was put down by the government without bloodshed.

The Second World War

Germany and the Soviet Union signed a non-aggression pact in August 1939. In a secret protocol to this pact, Finland was allotted to the Soviet sphere of influence. After the Finns had rejected Soviet territorial demands, the Soviet Union rescinded the 1932 non-aggression pact between the countries, and invaded Finland on November 30, 1939, starting the Winter War. The war ended

Independent Finland concluded a highly advantageous peace treaty with Soviet Russia in 1920. In the early '20s, Finland pursued cooperation with the "fringe states" Estonia, Latvia, Lithuania and Poland. The League of Nations was the cornerstone of Finnish security policy from the early 1920s to 1935, when the Finns adopted a new, Scandinavian orientation.

▲ In addition to imposing territorial concessions, the 1947 Treaty of Paris obliged Finland to pay the Soviet Union 300 million dollars' worth of war reparations. The reparations were paid off in the form of industrial goods, mainly metal products. Finland was the only country to pay off its war reparations in full. The last trainload of goods was sent off to the Soviet Union in 1952.

with the signing of the Treaty of Moscow on March 13, 1940, in which the Soviet Union gained southeastern Finland.

Seeking to boost its security after the Winter War, Finland gradually moved closer to Germany. When Germany attacked the Soviet Union on 22 June 1941, Finland first declared that it was neutral, but after the Soviets had bombed several Finnish cities, the government drew the conclusion that Finland was in a state of war. This conflict, known as the Continuation War, ended in a truce in September 1944. In addition to the previously ceded territory, Finland had to give up the Petsamo corridor, its only access to the Arctic Ocean. Some 420 000 refugees were moved to Finland from the ceded territory, primarily Karelia. The terms of the truce were confirmed in the Treaty of Paris, signed in 1947.

From Paasikivi to Kekkonen

Towards the end of the war, Marshal Mannerheim, commander-in-chief of the Army, was elected President of the Republic. He was succeeded in 1946 by J.K. Paasikivi, whose first objective was to establish friendly relations with the Soviet Union. The two countries concluded a Treaty on Friendship, Co-operation and Mutual Assistance in 1948, forming the basis for a policy that became known as the Paasikivi Line.

Over the next few years, Finland's international standing gradually strengthened. The Olympic Games were held in Helsinki in 1952, and that same year the last delivery of Finland's war reparations to the Soviet Union crossed the border.

The "spirit of Geneva" brought a thaw in world politics in the mid 1950s. In 1955 the Soviet Union announced that it would relinquish its lease on Porkkala, a tract of land west of Helsinki, that it had leased as a naval base since 1944. In the same spirit, Finland received a signal from the east that it was free to join the Nordic Council, a forum for inter-Nordic cooperation. Parliament passed a Government bill on joining this body in autumn 1955, and Finland was already represented at the Council's 1956 meeting in Copenhagen. This marked the beginning of Finland's full-fledged participation in Nordic cooperation. Its landmark achievements were the 1954 agreement on a common labour market and the abolition of passport controls between the Nordic countries in 1957.

Already back in 1947, Finland had applied for membership in the United Nations by a unanimous Parliament decision. With the Cold War at its height, however, the Soviet Union had vetoed Finland's membership at every vote. In 1955, however, Finland was admitted as a member along with 15 other states. Finland's neutrality dictated a conspicuously cautious voting behaviour in the UN on all matters involving conflict between the great powers. Thus, Finland abstained more frequently than its Nordic neighbours, although it generally followed a joint Nordic line in the UN.

Despite this cautious approach, Finland was actively involved in UN peacekeeping operations from the start, sending voluntary observers to Suez in November 1956.

Urho Kekkonen was first elected President in 1956 and he remained in office until autumn 1981. His aim was to increase Finland's room for manoeuvre in international affairs by pursuing an active policy of neutrality, taking the form of numerous initiatives on the international arena.

▼ Finland **joined** the European Union on 1 January 1995. The photo shows the European Commission representation in Helsinki.

SCIENTISTS AND EXPLORERS

Pehr Kalm (1716–1779) was appointed professor of economics at the Academy of Turku in 1747. That same year he set off on a four-year expedition to North America. The multi-volume account of his travels, translated into German, English and Dutch during his lifetime, made him an international celebrity.

Adolf Erik Nordenskiöld (1832–1901) was the father of Finnish mineralogy and an internationally renowned explorer. Having given up an attempt to reach the North Pole, in 1878–79 he became the first man to sail the Northeast Passage, the sea route following the north coast of Eurasia from Norway to the Bering Straits.

Edvard Westermarck (1862–1939) was a world-famous sociologist, who held a professorship in both Finland and Britain. His principal research themes are shown by the titles of two of his chief works, *The History of Human Marriage* (1891) and *The Origin and Development of Morals* (1906–1908). He carried out his most thoroughgoing field studies in Morocco.

A. I. Virtanen (1895–1973) was the father of Finnish biochemistry. He was a professor at the University of Helsinki from 1931 to 1948, when he became a member of the Academy of Finland. In 1945 he was awarded the Nobel Prize for Chemistry for a special fodder conservation method he had developed.

Georg Henrik von Wright (b. 1916) is one of the leading philosophers of the 20th century. He has served as professor at the universities of Helsinki, Cambridge and Cornell, and has been a member of the Academy of Finland since 1961. He has studied deontic logic, i.e. the logic of norms and ethics. Perhaps the best-known of his books is *Explanation and Understanding* (1971).

A CHRONOLOGY OF FINNISH HISTORY

8000–7000 B.C.	First signs of human habitation in present-day Finnish territory.
1155	The Swedes' First Crusade to the southwest coast of Finland.
1238	The Swedes' Second Crusade to Häme.
1293	The Swedes' Third Crusade to the end of the Gulf of Finland.
1323	Sweden and Novgorod conclude the Treaty of Pähkinäsaari. The eastern border of Finland is drawn for the first time.
1548	Mikael Agricola translates the New Testament into Finnish.
1550	Founding of Helsinki.
1640	Founding of the Academy of Turku (precursor of the present-day University of Helsinki).
1721	Sweden and Russia conclude the Treaty of Uusikaupunki.

1776	The first newspaper in Finnish is published.
1808	Russian invasion of Finland.
1809	Sweden and Russia conclude the Treaty of Hamina. Russia annexes Finland.
1812	Helsinki becomes the capital of Finland.
1835	The *Kalevala*, the Finnish national epic, is published.
1860	Finland obtains its own currency, the *markka*.
1863	The Language Manifesto. Finnish is to gain equivalent status with Swedish within 20 years.

In 1816, the German architect Carl Ludvig Engel was commissioned by the Tsar to design the centre of Helsinki, the new capital of the Grand Duchy. Engel produced an elegant blend of Berlin Neo-Classicism and St Petersburg tradition. Senate Square is still flanked, as in the drawing from left to right, by the University, the University Library and St Nicholas' Church (now the Cathedral). Only the guardhouse in front of the church has been demolished and replaced by broad stairs.

1863	The Diet begins to convene on a regular basis.
1878	Compulsory military service introduced. Finland obtains its own army.
1899–1905	First period of "Russification".
1907	Finland obtains a unicameral parliament, the *eduskunta*.
1909–1917	Second period of "Russification".
1917	Finland declares independence on December 6.
1918	Civil war breaks out on January 28.
1919	Republican form of government. K.J. Ståhlberg is elected President.
1920	Peace treaty concluded between Finland and Soviet Russia.
1921	Compulsory education enacted.
1922	Compulsory military service enacted.
1932	Prohibition repealed.
1932	Finland and Soviet Union sign non-aggression pact.
1939	Soviet Union attacks Finland on November 30; Winter War begins.
1940	Winter War ends with the Treaty of Moscow on March 13.
1941–1944	Continuation War between Finland and Soviet Union.
1946	J.K. Paasikivi elected President.
1952	Olympic Games in Helsinki.
1955	Finland joins the Nordic Council.
1955	Finland joins the United Nations.
1956	Urho Kekkonen elected President.
1982	Mauno Koivisto elected President.
1989	Finland becomes member of the Council of Europe.
1994	Martti Ahtisaari elected President.
1995	Finland becomes member of the European Union on January 1.
2000	Tarja Halonen elected President.
2002	Introduction of the euro.

The 1952 Olympic Games of Helsinki have been called the last genuine sports festival.

Throughout Kekkonen's presidency, however, the ever-darkening shadow of the Soviet Union lay over Finland, giving rise to the term "finlandization", first used abroad, but later in Finland, too.

New initiatives

Mauno Koivisto was elected president in 1982. He was succeeded in 1994 by Martti Ahtisaari, the first Finnish head of state to be elected by direct popular vote. Tarja Halonen was elected president in 2000, the first woman to hold this office.

The major upheavals set in motion in the late 1980s, ending the division of Europe and leading to the collapse of the Soviet Union, were reflected in Finland as a freeing of the psychological climate and greater latitude in foreign policy. The nation began to assert itself and take new international initiatives. In 1989 the country finally joined the Council of Europe, and in 1995 it became a member of the European Union. Finland adopted the euro in January 2002.

Northern
Democracy

The State

The historical foundation of Finland was the Scandinavian yeoman farmer's society. It is the only republic to have developed on this basis; and yet the Finnish President has a far greater political role than the monarchs of the other Scandinavian countries.

Finland is a democracy with parliamentary representation. Political power is vested in the people and wielded by the Parliament. Parliament is the supreme legislative body comprising 200 members elected for a four-year term. In addition to its role as legislator, Parliament has extensive powers to supervise the Government's actions in preparing decisions taken by the European Union and in formulating Finland's position.

The Finnish Constitution guarantees to all citizens extensive individual rights corresponding to those enumerated in the UN Declaration of Human Rights. The status of the Swedish-speaking minority is guaranteed in the Constitution and in the Language Act, its offshoot: in practice, this status is problem-free. Citizens are free to conduct their official business in either Finnish or Swedish, as they prefer. There has been no tension between the language groups for many decades now.

▼ The governments formed in 1995 and 1999 were both based on the same coalition between the Social Democrats, the Conservatives, the Swedish People's Party, the Left Alliance and the Greens. The leaders of the two principal Government parties are Prime Minister Paavo Lipponen (right) and Minister of Finance Sauli Niinistö. In charge since Finland's accession to the EU, they guided the country into joining the economic and monetary union (EMU).

Valtiovarainministeri
Sauli Niinistö

Pääministeri
Paavo Lipponen

◀ Many farmers today have diversified from traditional agriculture. Thus, many farms run shops offering their own produce and other goods besides. Farm tourism provides a welcome source of additional income.

The President

The head of state is the President of the Republic, elected by direct popular vote for a six-year term. The President directs Finland's foreign and security policy jointly with the Government. The Government nominates and the President appoints and dismisses ministers and leading civil servants, judges and officers. The President is also commander-in-chief of the defence forces. The President submits Government bills to Parliament, and ratifies Acts of Parliament and approves decrees on their implementation as well as on administrative matters. Although not directly answerable to Parliament, the President must rely on the support of the Government, which in turn must have Parliament's confidence. In theory the supreme guardian of the administration, in practice the President always bases his or her decisions on the proposal of the competent minister; these decisions only acquire the force of law once ratified by the minister in question.

Leadership of foreign and security policy was for many years the President's most important prerogative. Its constitutional definition remained unchanged until the year 2000, although in practice the President's power varied according to Finland's security policy situation and the political personality of the incumbent.

In the years between the wars, presidents hardly ever asserted their powers in foreign policy. This was partly because Finland steered clear of international crises, but also because the early incumbents were either passive in the foreign policy field or politically weak.

At the time the Winter War (1939–40) broke out, the President was old and ailing. The real power was in the hands of the three most powerful members of the Government. By 1941, when the Continuation War broke out, a new President was in office. Though forceful, active and intelligent, the President shared leadership in the country's foreign policy with the charismatic and highly popular Marshal C.G.E. Mannerheim, to whom he had surrendered command of the army.

During the Cold War, the fundamental problem of Finnish security policy was how to defend against the ideological and political expansionism of the Soviet Union. The balance between tactical appeasement and strategic self-defence depended at all times on the personal contribution of the President.

During this period the presidents – J.K. Paasikivi followed by Urho Kekkonen – kept an iron grip on Finland's foreign policy, relying on their personal authority. Kekkonen remained in office for 25 years. During this period, his inner circle gradually gained an increasingly powerful role alongside the Government. Its influence was exercised by means of statements issued either directly by the President or by his intermediaries. This arrangement was necessary to reassure the Soviet Union; in it there were also, however, elements of a struggle for domination of domestic policy on the part of the President and his closest associates. This linking up of foreign and domestic policy ended with the Kekkonen era in the early 1980s.

▼ Tarja Halonen was elected Finland's first woman president in spring 2000. Here she poses with her predecessors Mauno Koivisto (left) and Martti Ahtisaari (right) at the Independence Day (December 6) reception in the President's Palace in Helsinki.

FINLAND'S PRESIDENTS

K. J. Ståhlberg	1919–1925
L. Kr. Relander	1925–1931
P. E. Svinhufvud	1931–1937
Kyösti Kallio	1937–1940
Risto Ryti	1940–1944
C. G. E. Mannerheim	1944–1946
J. K. Paasikivi	1946–1956
Urho Kekkonen	1956–1982
Mauno Koivisto	1982–1994
Martti Ahtisaari	1994–2000
Tarja Halonen	2000–

At this time, the locus of power in security matters began to shift to the Government. The transition advanced gradually, with occasional lapses, in the 1980s during the presidency of Mauno Koivisto, but accelerated after he was succeeded by Martti Ahtisaari in the 1990s. When Finland joined the European Union, the Constitution was amended to transfer the responsibility for foreign and security policy decisions to be made within the Union from the President to the Prime Minister, thus bringing them under parliamentary control. Owing to our country's long presidential tradition, this change has been slow to take effect.

The Constitution

The Finnish Constitution has proved exceptionally long-lived. The Constitution Act (*hallitusmuoto*), which lays down the roles and balance of power between the Parliament, Government and President, survived both the Second World War and the Cold War. The national election system and the Parliament Act (*valtiopäiväjärjestys*), on which parliamentary procedure is based, date back to the years before the First World War. The essential elements of these old constitutional laws have been consolidated in the current Constitution.

The constitutional democracy functioned virtually without a hitch even during Finland's war against the Soviet Union in the days of the Second World War. Apart from Britain, Finland was the only country to have taken part in the Second World War in which postwar reconstruction could begin on the basis of a constitution enacted before the war.

The strong constitutional position of the President was initially due to the situation in Finland just after the country became independent in 1917. Following the Civil War of 1918, it was felt that to prevent further unrest, a strong executive was needed. Some of the presidential powers actually derived from the old Constitution adopted in the late 18th century, during the last years of Swedish rule. The key constitutional provisions remained in force throughout the period of Russian rule (1809–1917).

For a long time, the President had the right to dissolve Parliament in mid-term, but this right was exercised on only a very few occasions, most recently in the mid 1970s. The right of initiative in the dissolution of Parliament was transferred in the early '90s to the Prime Minister. At the same time, the opposition was deprived of the possibility of voting by a qualified minority to shelve a bill until after the next elections. Following the introduction of the normal parliamentary system of majority voting, most governments have been based on a broad coalition and have remained in power throughout the election period.

The new Constitution that came into force in 2000 gave the parliamentary groups a still more prominent role in ministerial appointments. The President's power to decide on appointments of senior civil servants was also curtailed. The President retains the right to issue decrees, but this power depends more directly than before on Government approval. The President's leading role in security policy has also diminished.

The main aim of the new Constitution was to consolidate the constitutional provisions previously included in several different acts into one single act. Most of the amendments introduced were relatively minor, but their overall impact contributed to strengthening the status of the Prime Minister and thus of Parliament.

In principle, this means that the formal powers of the President will diminish slightly. The ceremonial and symbolic significance of the presidency is so strong, however, that the President will remain the leading force in the Finnish political system. The influence of the President in the future is likely to depend more on intellectual and moral leadership and media skills than on the formal powers conferred by the Constitution.

The political parties

Finland has had a system of general and equal suffrage since 1906, which is also when women received the vote. Over one third of all MPs are women. The voting age is 18.

The three biggest parties dominate the political scene. Following the civil war (fought right after Finland became independent), the Social Democratic Party steered the labour movement in the direction of a Western-type

▼ The power belongs to the people. The people's elected delegates electing Finland's first president, K.J. Ståhlberg.

▲ Around the turn of the century, many associations advocated general and equal suffrage, which meant that women, too, should have the right to vote. Legislation to this effect was passed in 1906. Here, the constitutive meeting of the Finnish Working Women's Association, 1900.

democracy. During the years of uncertainty following the Second World War, the Social Democrats were the mainstay of the struggle against Soviet pressure and the communist bid for power. The Social Democrats are backed financially and ideologically by the powerful labour unions. The Centre Party, which originally represented rural interests, has retained a strong position even though the relative size of the agricultural population has long been as low as on the Continent. The conservative National Coalition is the third major political force, having developed from a middle-class urban party in the direction of a nationwide white-collar workers' party.

The three main parties are followed by three midsize parties. The Left-Wing Alliance occupies the vacuum that arose as a result of the exit of the Communist Party from the political arena. The Greens first appeared on the political scene in the early 1980s, and have gradually consolidated their position. They have been represented in the Government since the late 1990s. The Swedish People's Party defends the interests of the speakers of Finland's minority language; its representation in Parliament is roughly the same as the ratio of Swedish-speakers to the overall population.

In addition to those mentioned above, there are generally from two to four smaller parties in Parliament, some of them the last survivors of political movements that are losing momentum, others pioneers of new, rising parties.

The parliamentary elections of 1999

The Social Democrats were hard hit towards the end of the 1995–99 parliamentary term by a financial scandal in which the party's former chairman was implicated.

Unemployment had decreased markedly during the past term, and disposable income of households had grown slowly but surely. The economic outlook was favourable.

The Social Democrats lost 12 seats, but retained their position as the largest party. The Centre Party gains were smaller than expected, as the party platform's call for restricting the power of the trade unions scared off many voters who preferred security to radical change. The Conservative Party chairman won a record number of votes in Helsinki, but the Conservatives still won fewer seats than the Centre Party. The Centre Party chairman Esko Aho was runner-up to Tarja Halonen in a very tight race for the presidency of Finland in 2000. The basic political composition of the government remained unchanged.

Parliament

Under the Constitution, Parliament is the supreme branch of government. In practice, however, parliamentary legislation and other decision-making tends to be based on Government proposals. The country's general political direction is laid down in the Government programme, drawn up after parliamentary elections when the cabinet is formed. The Government measures the degree of confidence it enjoys in Parliament by submitting its programme for debate in Parliament.

Government bills are drafted and presented to the ministers by senior civil servants of the various ministries.The bills are then submitted to Parliament. In theory, Parliament is free to amend these texts as a result of its debates in committee and plenary sessions; the Finnish political tradition, however, is such that Parliament rarely tampers with the substance of Government bills.

In practice, all parliamentary groups included in the government coalition are bound by the decisions agreed on by the ministers concerning texts drafted by the civil service. In recent years, however, the parliamentary groups have shown signs of adopting a more active approach: even MPs of Government parties have proposed Parliament amendments to Government bills, and have pushed them through, too.

▶ Parliament has 200 members, of whom more than one third were women during the 1999–2003 term. There are also several women ministers in the Cabinet.

Every Government bill is debated three times by the full Parliament. Following a preliminary debate in plenary session, the bill is referred to the appropriate committee. An often quite extensive series of hearings ensues, during which the background and impact of the bill are examined in detail. Committee meetings are closed to the public. Debates in committee often have a real impact on individual positions, and are only in part tied to political affiliations.

The committee report is presented at the first reading, which goes on to debate it and decide on amendments to its contents. Individual MPs may here propose further amendments to the text, but it is very rare for such changes to be adopted. At the second reading, Parliament decides whether or not to adopt the bill.

Before coming into force, an Act of Parliament must be confirmed by the President. If the President refuses to confirm the Act and sends it back, Parliament can override the President by voting to adopt the Act without changes.

Members of Parliament may also propose for adoption by Parliament a new Act or an amendment to existing provisions. Government bills, however, must be dealt with first. Acts based on MP initiatives are very rarely adopted; recently no more than two or three times per parliamentary term.

A Parliamentary question hour is held weekly, and frequently broadcast live to the nation. Members may make oral questions to the Ministers, who must respond immediately. MPs may

◀ The Finns are more cautious about resorting to industrial action than many other nations. This picket's sign reads "Even nurses should be paid".

also submit written questions to the Government on any matter of their choice. The Minister responsible must provide a written answer within three weeks.

The social partners

The labour and management organizations concluded the first comprehensive collective agreement in the late 1960s, laying down the guidelines for agreements in all the different sectors. In addition to wages and other working conditions, such agreements include provisions on taxation and social policy. Collective bargaining has now settled into a well-established pattern, with the Government playing an increasingly important mediating role in the talks. The "tripartite" agreement reached with this method formally binds only the labour and management organizations involved, but in practice it is final: if Parliament were to enact legislation conflicting with the tripartite agreement, the result would be a serious political crisis. The organizations have therefore gradually taken over some of the power originally vested in Parliament, although a Parliament decision is still required to bring the agreements formally into force.

The powerful negotiating position of the employees' organizations is based on Finland's exceptionally high degree of organized labour: over 80% of the workforce are union members. The pressure for joining a union is strong, as earnings-related unemployment benefits are only paid to members of an unemployment insurance association, the largest of which are run by the unions. The membership fees are deducted by the employer and paid direct to the unions. If more than half the employees in a sector are union members, collective agreements in that sector also cover non-members.

General political trends

From the early years of independence right up to the Cold War period, Finland's governments tended to be short-lived. It was quite common for talks to begin on the composition and programme of the next government as soon as a new government was sworn in. With economic progress and a more peaceful social climate, governments have become more enduring. From the 1980s, they have stayed in power for the full four-year parliamentary term.

In recent decades, governments have been formed in coalition by two of the three main parties, generally with the support of the Swedish People's Party. The government of Paavo Lipponen, which came into power in the latter half of the 1990s, has the broadest political base seen to date, consisting of the Social Democrats and the conservative National Coalition together with the Left-Wing Alliance, the Swedish People's Party and the Greens. For the first time in Finnish history, the conservatives and the extreme left thus sit in the same Cabinet; and the Green League also made history by being the first European environmental party to enter a national government.

During the Cold War, the President alone was responsible for defining and implementing the basic lines of foreign and security policy. The President tended to see the Foreign Minister as his personal aide-de-camp. The removal of the Soviet threat and membership of the European Union have led to a normalization of security policy. The foreign policy role of the Prime Minister has strengthened and the *de facto* influence of the President has diminished. The new Constitution com-

◀ Harri Holkeri, former Prime Minister of Finland, has acted as Independent Chairman of the Northern Ireland Talks Process. Here, Holkeri holding up the Shamrock Award. Holkeri also served as President of the UN General Assembly in 2000.

mits the President more tightly than before to the Government line in foreign and security policy.

Almost as soon as it had taken office in spring 1995, the first Lipponen Government presented Parliament with an extensive report defining a new orientation for Finnish security policy. In it Finland gave up the neutrality guarded so jealously throughout the Cold War.

The security policy report redefined Finland's international position on the basis of EU membership, military non-alignment and an independent defence. The Parliament debated the report in two sessions, each lasting several days. Previously, the security policy had been determined by the President alone, and during the Cold War no-one had even dared to put it down in writing. Now Parliament debated the policy in public and required an undertaking from the Government to present a new proposal to Parliament as soon as there was any need to modify the approved policy.

The Government adopted the same parliamentary procedure in requesting authorization for Finnish troops to participate in UN peacekeeping operations in former Yugoslavia. Two years after the report on security policy, the Government submitted for Parliament approval a basic document on the goals of Finland's defence policy and the structure and function of the Defence Forces.

In 1990, the public debt was only about 10% of gross domestic product. Then recession set in, with soaring unemployment and a bank crisis which rocked the very foundation of the financial system. The public finances were undermined by overly generous unemployment benefits and welfare. Finland had a serious budget deficit throughout the early '90s, and the net debt continued to grow even when the economy was beginning to recover. The government did not succeed in balancing the budget again until the late 1990s.

Administration

The Government currently consists of the Prime Minister and 17 other ministers. The administration comprises 12 sectoral ministries. Ministers have extensive independent powers to run their ministries and subordinate agencies. The Government bills submitted to Parliament are drafted in the ministries.

Local government

Finland is divided administratively into four provinces and 448 municipalities (local authorities). The latter are required by law to provide welfare services. Their main source of income is from the municipal tax, a standard rate levied on income and collected in conjunction with the progressive State income tax. The State also pays the local authorities to provide welfare services. This sum, known as the 'State share' is calculated in proportion to population and accounts for some 40 per cent of local government income.

The local authorities decide independently on how best to produce the required services with the funds at their disposal. The main services for which they are responsible are health care and hospitals, basic education, social services, fire-fighting and rescue services. They also maintain a library system which covers the whole country and is among the most effective in the world. The local authorities have wide-ranging powers in physical planning. The maintenance of local infrastructure is in part organized along profit-making business principles. This applies to water supply and sewerage and in part to heat and electricity generation and the operation of ports.

The local authorities lay down their own municipal tax rate on the basis of their needs for financing the required services. The rate ranges from 16 to 20 per cent. Political decisions on taxation, finance, administration and town planning are taken by the municipal council. Council elections, based on universal and equal suffrage, are held every four years. In addition to Finnish citizens, foreigners who are permanent residents in the municipality may vote.

The local branches of the main parliamentary parties dominate Finnish local politics, but many councils feature substantial independent groups. A large proportion of MPs are also municipal councillors, and many of them hold leadership positions in local government.

Åland self-government

The Åland Islands in the northern Baltic Sea enjoy special status, having been declared a demilitarized zone by international treaty. Historically, the roots of this status go back to the Crimean War fought in the mid nineteenth century. The islands' international position and autonomy were confirmed in the Åland Self-Government Act. Passed in the 1920s, this act enshrines the linguistic and cultural rights of Åland's Swedish-speaking population. The central government is represented by a Governor appointed by the President of the Republic, but the day-to-day business of government in the islands is handled by the Åland Provincial Assembly, elected by popular vote.

Residents of mainland Finland are not entitled to own land in Åland.

▼ Finnish libraries have kept up with the times by making use of new digital aids. Lending figures for traditional books are still high, nonetheless. In this country of 5.2 million inhabitants, the average Finn borrows 20 books a year.

The men of Åland are exempted from compulsory military service, instead of which they may opt to serve in the lighthouse and pilot service run by the province's civilian government. Under Finland's Treaty of Accession to the European Union, there is a customs border between Åland and the mainland, and the same rules apply to trade across this border as those which apply to trade between Finland and non-EU countries.

▼ The Finnish court system is three-tiered. The district courts deal with both criminal cases and civil disputes. District court judgments can generally be appealed to one of the Appeals Courts, whose decisions can in turn be appealed to the Supreme Court of Justice, provided that the latter agrees to hear the case. There are a number of special courts, such as the Market Court and the Labour Court. Appeals of decisions taken by authorities are heard in the administrative courts and the Supreme Administrative Court.

The Courts

In accordance with the classic doctrine of the separation of powers, the Finnish judiciary is independent of the legislative and executive branches of government. Its only connection with the executive is that the President appoints the justices of the high courts. Thereafter they, like all other judges, are virtually undismissible. The court system is three-tiered. Only cases having the nature of a precedent or in which an obvious procedural error has been committed go all the way to the highest level. The constitution of ad hoc courts is forbidden. The prosecuting authority, headed by the State Prosecutor's Office, is independent of both the courts and the police.

In addition to the general courts, there are several specialized courts dealing, among other matters, with housing, insurance, water and market affairs. Administrative courts act as courts of appeal in matters of administrative procedure. Charges brought against a minister or one of the country's chief law officers are examined by the High Court of Impeachment. The

▲ The fighter aircraft used by the Finnish Air Force are the US Hornet and the UK Hawk.

decision to impeach a minister is made by Parliament, but the conditions to be met are so stringent that impeachment on political grounds is not possible. The Court of Impeachment has been convened only on a handful of occasions.

The Chancellor of Justice is the supreme guardian of legality. He/she attends all Government meetings and may intervene if there is a danger that the form or legal content of a decision may conflict with the law. Any citizen whose rights have been violated may submit a complaint to the Chancellor of Justice about the actions of the authorities. The Parliamentary Ombudsman supervises the legality of official actions and examines complaints by citizens; he/she is also responsible for monitoring the prison system and the defence forces.

Defence

The national defence is based on a system of regional defence networks covering the whole country. It is founded on the principle of compulsory military service for men. Every year, an age group of approximately 30 000 Finns is trained. This figure usually includes about 500 women, for whom military service is voluntary. The service period for conscripts trained for command posts is approximately one year, that for the rank and file six months.

The task of the training units is to produce manpower for the wartime army, in which each reservist has a specific task. The reserve troops are frequently called up for refresher courses, attended by 35,000 persons every year. The trained reserve forces are about half a million strong, or almost 10% of the entire population, which is the highest ratio of trained reservists in Europe.

Finland is prepared to mobilize 22 brigades armed for regional defence and three rapid deployment units armed for effective, mobile defence

aimed at the point of main effort. The wartime strength of the defence forces is 430,000 soldiers.

The Finnish Air Force is currently replacing its air fleet: its main aircraft as of the year 2000 are the American F-18 (Hornet) and the British Hawk fighter planes. The armoured vehicles of the land forces were originally made in the former Soviet Union and GDR, but retrofitted with Finnish signalling and fire control technology. The backbone of the coastal defence consists of Swedish-made marine target missiles based on fast battleships and land-based mobile launchpads, a highly developed sonar system and an effective mine system.

The concept of compulsory military service is widely backed by popular opinion. Opinion polls indicate that even during the Cold War, when Finland had an agreement with the Soviet Union containing provisions on defence policy cooperation, well over two thirds of the respondents were prepared to take up arms to defend their country in any contingency. During the 1990s this readiness to defend the country and the belief in Finland's defensive capability have increased markedly.

Finland is involved in the NATO Partnership for Peace programme and the Euro-Atlantic Partnership Council. Finnish peacekeeping troops have served on UN missions to Lebanon and Macedonia. A Finnish light infantry battalion took part in the SFOR operation in Bosnia and the KFOR operation in Kosovo under NATO command.

Although Finland's security policy is based on military neutrality, the Finns do not rule out the possibility of entering into an alliance. However, they generally have strong reservations about NATO membership.

The Church

The Catholic Church extended its hold over most of the Finnish population in the 12th century, when the Swedes conquered western Finland. Meanwhile, the Principality of Novgorod was busy propagating the Orthodox creed in Karelia and eastern Finland. The Lutheran doctrine of Reformation took over from the Catholic Church during the 16th century, since which Finland and the other Nordic countries have been the foremost stronghold of Lutheranism in the world.

In principle, the Finnish State is neutral in religious matters, but the Evangelical-Lutheran Church is mentioned in the Constitution Act, and its administration and activities, as well as those of the Finnish Orthodox Church,

are regulated by the Church Act, issued by Parliament. Both Churches have extensive autonomy, and their funding is secured by the right to levy a tax on their members. This in fact provides most of their income. Parishes keep population registers and are responsible for the upkeep of church buildings of cultural and historical value and of graveyards.

The Evangelical-Lutheran congregations had 4,410,000 members in 2000, or 85.1% of the population.

Several large and influential revivalist movements operate within the Church. They were established in the nineteenth century by charismatic lay preachers and priests. The archbishop's see is Turku. There are eight dioceses; all of the country's Swedish-speaking congregations belong to the diocese of Borgå (Porvoo).

The Evangelical-Lutheran Church comprises 586 parishes (2000), which have considerable financial and operational independence. The parishes are served by some 1,800 clergy, over one fifth of whom are women. The first women priests were ordained in 1988.

▼ The first Finnish women priests were ordained in 1988; there are no women bishops yet.

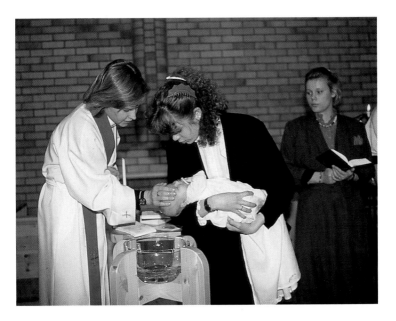

Finland's second largest religious community is the Orthodox Church, which has just under 56,000 members, or 1.1% of the population. The church is under the direct protection of the patriarchate of Constantinople. The archbishop's see is Kuopio, and there are three dioceses: Helsinki, Karelia and Oulu.

The Pentecostal revival movement includes some 50,000 baptized members plus a considerable number of their children. Jehovah's Witnesses have over 18,000 members in Finland, the Free Church of Finland has 13,000, the Catholic Church 7,000 and the Jewish congregations 1,100 members. The number of Muslims has increased more than tenfold over the last ten years, but only a handful – about 1,200 – are registered as members of official religious communities.

Over 660,000 Finns, or 12.7% of the population, are classified as non-denominational. During the 1990s, the number of people leaving the Church slightly exceeded those joining it. There are few atheists, however, as half of those who are not members of a church consider themselves to be Christians.

The average member of the Church attends divine service twice a year. Although the Finns are thus rather infrequent churchgoers, polls indicate that almost half the population (well over half of the women and one third of the men) consider themselves believers. This proportion is highest among the oldest age groups.

The Economy

The Finnish economy has gone through two complete metamorphoses during the past few decades. First, this once predominantly agrarian country saw the swiftest process of industrialization and urbanization of any country in Europe. More recently, the production of high technology has proliferated, while the traditional smokestack industries have been subjected to wholesale rationalization and internationalization. In many cases, this has led to drastic changes in ownership arrangements. Economic policy became increasingly liberal as Finland struggled to overcome the depression that hit the country in the early 1990s.

These rapid transformations have naturally left their mark on Finnish society. Despite heavy unemployment, however, the country has remained remarkably stable. To be sure, the country will still need time and flexibility to adjust fully to structural changes.

Electronics to the fore

Growth has been fastest in the 1990s in the electronics industry. Finland's flagship company in the field is Nokia, although there are also a number of smaller, more specialized electronics firms. The more conventional electrotechnical industry is represented by the world's third largest lift manufacturer Kone and its offshoot KCI-Konecranes, and by ABB Strömberg, founded over a century ago by a Finnish pioneer of electrical engineering. The sector has been highly regarded in Finland

▶ Jorma Ollila, CEO, has every reason to be proud of his company. Nokia is one of the world's leading manufacturers of mobile phones and a linchpin of the Finnish economy.

FINLAND'S LARGEST INDUSTRIAL AND COMMERCIAL ENTERPRISES IN 2001

Name	Line of business	Turnover billion euro
1. Nokia	Electronics	31.2
2. Stora Enso	Forest industry	13.5
3. Fortum	Energy, oil	10.4
4. UPM-Kymmene	Forest industry	9.9
5. Metsäliitto (M-Real)	Forest industry	8.8
6. Kesko	Retail chain	6.2
7. Outokumpu	Metallurgy	5.3
8. Metso	Machinery	4.3
9. Tamro	Pharmaceuticals wholesalers	3.8
10. SOK	Retail chain	2.9

Source: *Helsingin Sanomat 12.3.* 2002.

ever since 1887, when young Gottfried Strömberg was appointed lecturer in electrical engineering at the institution today known as the Helsinki University of Technology (cf. the chapter *Scientific feats*).

Of course Finland does not have natural features that particularly favour the growth of the electrical industry – if, indeed, any country has such features. A possible advantage, however, is the fact that the sector does not depend heavily on raw materials.

Nokia, one of Finland's industrial giants since the 1860s, began to take an interest in electronics in the 1960s as an offshoot of its cable manufacturing operations. In the 1970s the company took over the industrial operations of the national telecommunications administration. In the 1980s the group began to specialize, buying up several electronics firms in Sweden, Germany and elsewhere.

Falling on hard times, Nokia gave up its forest operations, rubber and cable manufacturing and the production of TV sets and computers. The proliferation of cellular phones in the mid 1990s gave Nokia a new lease on life. The company has continually developed its mobile technology and is now the world leader in the sector.

Previously owned by Finnish commercial banks and other institutions, Nokia (like many other major Finnish companies) now has increasingly international ownership arrangements. The lift maker Kone, however, is still controlled by the Herlin family. Its new top-of-the-line product is a lift without an engine room. Strömberg, now a subsidiary of ABB (Asea Brown Boveri), has concentrated successfully on manufacturing heavy electrical machinery.

▲ Kone is the world's third biggest manufacturer of lifts and escalators. The company is now marketing its innovative lift without an engine room, which is likely to lead to new applications for elevator technology.

Specialized metal products

The metal products sector, which includes both electrical equipment and electronics, is Finland's leading export industry today in terms of both volume of production and jobs.

It is a byword in the business that the Finns are good at making anything "bigger than a horse". We have little chance of competing with standardized products, such as domestic appliances, which require large production volumes. On the other hand, Finland can be successful in making sophisticated specialized technology, such as state-of-the-art electronics and large-scale industrial systems. A high-tech approach also underlies the very successful Oras water tap.

Not surprisingly, Finland is a leading manufacturer of machinery for the timber and wood-processing industries. Expertise in paper machines is today concentrated in the hands of Valmet, originally set up as the national arms factory. It has merged with a number of private engineering works (Rauma, Tampella and others), forming the Metso group, which produces all of Finland's paper machines. Related operations are handled by Jaakko Pöyry, one of the world's leading paper industry consultancies. The Partek

▲ Oras taps control water temperature with the push of a button.

group (soon to merge with Kone), a former cement company, now makes Multilift loading equipment and Valtra tractors. Finland is also a world leader on the forest machine market.

The worldwide shipyard crisis has also affected Finland, but the Norwegian-owned Kvaerner Masa-Yards has had considerable success in building luxury cruisers. Aker Finnyards at Rauma also makes cruisers.

Icebreakers, Finland's traditional forte, are still going strong. Wärtsilä, a

subsidiary of Metra, is now a leading manufacturer of diesel engines for ships and power plants. Another major engineering firm is Tamrock, which makes mining equipment and other heavy machinery.

The metallurgical industry has had to adjust, as domestic mining operations have petered off in the past few years. The Outokumpu company has therefore acquired copper plants and other metal works around the world. The flash smelting method, developed by Outokumpu, is a major Finnish industrial invention. The company's special steels production has been divested to an affiliated group, AvestaPolarit. Rautaruukki is a successful steel company. Previously State-owned, both Outokumpu and Rautaruukki have been privatized.

Living on forests

Finland has traditionally "lived on her forests". The paper industry is still a vital source of exports. Finland is also a major global player in the sawmill and board sector and other mechanical wood-processing industries. The forest industry needs little imported input, which boosts Finland's balance of payments.

The forest industry today is highly automated; a 100-metre paper machine is operated by a handful of controllers sitting at their screens. The enormous investments required have resulted in intense concentration. To begin with, the Finnish companies in the paper sector formed three groups; then they merged with other Nordic companies; and finally they went global.

The 125-year-old Enso group, in which the Finnish government bought a majority share in 1918, merged in 1998 with the Swedish company Stora Kopperberg, which itself dates all the

way back to the Middle Ages. The resulting Stora Enso subsequently bought up the American family company Consolidated Papers. UPM-Kymmene, formed as the result of a merger of numerous smaller Finnish paper companies, is also actively looking for opportunities for further expansion.

Stora Enso and UPM-Kymmene are among the largest paper manufacturers in the world, alongside the American International Papers. The majority share in the third large Finnish paper group, Metsäliitto and M-Real, remains in the hands of tens of thousands of ordinary Finnish forest owners. Myllykoski, a smaller but highly international company, is still a family business.

The wood-processing industry has boosted its ecological impact radically since the 1970s. The modern pulp mill is virtually a closed circuit; its process water is cleaned up and recycled, while waste is incinerated, making the mill self-sufficient in terms of energy. The production of mechanical pulp (groundwood) for newsprint and other paper, however, still requires a great deal of electricity. Finland meticulously recycles its waste paper.

▲ Metso's new Valmet paper machine combines technological know-how from many fields into new processes.

Forests owned by farmers

Finland's vast forests are primarily (54%) in private ownership. The owners are farmers or, increasingly, their citified descendants. Hundreds of thousands of Finns are forest owners. About one third of all forests (mainly in northern Finland) belong to the government, while the wood-processing companies own less than 10%. The situation differs radically from that in other countries. This fragmentation causes some problems with felling; on the other hand, the owners naturally take good care of their inherited woodlands, some of which have been in the family for centuries.

The volume of forest growth has exceeded the volume felled in Finland since the 1960s. Thus there is probably more wood in the Finnish forests than ever before. The authorities see to it that reforestation begins immediately after a stand of trees is felled. Trees reach full harvesting size in about 70 years – a great deal faster in the southern parts of the country than in Lap-

◀ The panorama windows of the Timberjack harvester make it easy for the operator to keep an eye on his progress.

land. Large-scale clear cutting is prohibited.

Forestry methods are much debated in Finland. A powerful harvester may not be a beautiful sight, but who would be prepared these days to set off into the forest with a saw and an axe and to drag the logs through deep snow to the nearest river, as 300 000 men still did back in the 1950s? Today there are only a few thousand lumberjacks left. If it had not been for the rational use of forests, there never would have been a Finnish nation.

Chemicals and energy

The basic chemicals industry in Finland is largely in the hands of two companies originally set up by the government. Kemira's main products include fertilizers and paints, while Neste (now part of Fortum) refines oil and distributes natural gas. Plastic products are made by e.g. Perlos and Uponor.

The Finnish building materials industry dwindled during the 1990s. Joint Nordic arrangements have been concluded for the cement sector. The construction sector proper includes both Finnish companies and international competitors.

Electricity was previously generated by State-run companies, industry and municipally-owned power plants. Deregulation has brought turmoil to the sector: Finnish and Swedish energy conglomerates have bought up small local power companies, and the State-owned Imatran Voima has been merged into the Fortum group.

Despite its almost 200 000 lakes, Finland is a low-lying country, and hydroelectric power is relatively scarce. Nonetheless, the Finns have decided to refrain from harnessing their last free-flowing rapids. On the other hand, Finland is a leader in the production of highly efficient back-pressure power and district heating. Nuclear energy, a subject of much debate, covers 18% of the country's overall energy requirement. Increasing use is being made of natural gas imported from Russia. The peat won from Finland's extensive wetlands is also used locally for power generation.

KEY ECONOMIC STATISTICS
(mainly 2000)

HOUSING
- total number of homes   2.5   million
- average size   77   sq. m.
- space per person   35   sq.m.
- owner-occupied   58%

ENERGY SOURCES
- oil   27%
- papermaking
  processes etc.   21%
- nuclear   18%
- coal   11%
- natural gas   11%
- hydroelectric   4%
- peat   4%
- imported energy   3%

Total energy consumption:
  1307 terajoules

ECONOMY (2001)
- gross domestic product   135 billion euro
- taxes of GDP   46%
- per capita income   21,340 euro
- unemployment rate   9%
- EMU public debt   59 billion euro
- government budget   35 billion euros
    (year 2002)
- inflation rate   2.6%

TRANSPORT
- private cars   2.1   million
- roads   77,900   km
- railway tracks   5,854   km
- airline passengers   13.9   million
- fixed line telephones   2.8   million
- mobile telephones   3.7   million

AGRICULTURE
- number of farms (over 1 ha)   78.890
- average size of fields   28 hectares
- yield per hectare (wheat)   3.6 tonnes
- self-sufficiency rate (cereals)   103%
    (only 40% in 1999)
- head of livestock   1.1 million

FORESTRY
- farmed forest 26.3 million hectares

- ownership: private 54%, government
  33%, companies 8%, other 5%

- tree species (by volume): pine 47%,
  spruce 34%, deciduous species 19%

- annual growth of trees: 78 million
  cubic metres; commercial felling:
  65 million cubic metres (considerable
  annual fluctuation)

INDUSTRY

	Jobs	Value added billion euro
Metal products	118,873	5.9
Electronics	66,536	7.9
Food	39,775	1.8
Paper	37,403	5.5
Chemicals	40,031	3.1
Graphic industry	31,045	1.6
Mechanical wood-working	28,494	1.4
Power plants etc.	17,055	2.0
Metallurgy	16,894	1.4
Cement, ceramics	15,356	0.9
Textiles	14,625	0.5
Furniture	11,689	0.5
Mining	4,287	0.2
Total	446,443	33.1

Workforce
- services   66%
- industry and construction   27%
- agriculture   6%

Total 2.4 million employed, 231.000 unemployed

Food and design

The basic foodstuffs industry was protected by high tariffs until Finland joined the European Union in 1995, opening the floodgates for full-scale competition. The result was a major restructuring of the domestic food-processing sector, although it remained basically in the hands of Finnish farmers. The company Raisio has gained an international reputation with its food fat called Benecol, which reduces blood cholesterol levels.

The Finnish food-processing industry is now busily establishing Nordic and Baltic partnerships. Some of the leading companies in the field are Fazer (confectionery), Paulig (coffee), Hartwall and Sinebrychoff (breweries) and Valio (dairy products). A Finnish company that has gone multinational is the Huhtamäki Group, which manufactures Polarcup packaging.

The leading Finnish pharmaceuticals firm Orion focuses on markets in the neighbouring countries, but has also developed a number of internationally successful trademark drugs. Leiras, a Finnish company that is now a subsidiary of Schering, is one of the world's leading producers of contraceptives.

The consumer goods industry in general has been strongly affected by growing international competition. Mass-produced goods are imported from countries with low production costs, while Finnish companies focus on specialized quality products. Clothes firms include Luhta (L-Fashion) and Marimekko.

The Hackman company is responsible for most of the production known generically as Finnish Design (Arabia porcelain and Iittala glassware, cf. the chapter on design by Kaija Valkonen). There are two large furniture manufacturers (Asko-Sotka and Isku) and several smaller ones. One of these is Artek, which sells furniture designed by Alvar Aalto.

Services

Until quite recently, Finland was essentially an agrarian country with a relatively undeveloped service sector. The rapid increase in earnings and tax rates over the last few decades has largely turned Finland into a self-service country. Moreover, many national and municipal services have been cut during the past few years.

The perishables market was long divided between four retail chains, but this situation has changed completely

▼ In these days of cheap imports, the Finnish textile industry must focus on quality to retain its market shares. In particular, sales of sportswear and other leisurewear are on the rise.

▶ New department stores, supermarkets and shopping malls are springing up constantly in towns and suburbs.

in the 1990s. The market is dominated by Kesko (K stores), owned by individual retailers, whereas the former wholesalers' T chain (which included Spar and Wihuri) has split up. After a successful restructuring operation, the cooperative S chain has grown fast, while the E chain, formerly run by the labour movement, is also recovering after a rocky patch. So far, foreign groups have played only a minor role on the Finnish retail market.

All these changes were dictated by the trend towards ever larger supermarkets and hypermarkets. Finland's largest department store is still Stockmann's.

The tourist sector has revived in recent years. Indeed, after a hiatus of 80 years, Finland is now seeing a spate of Russian tourists. The Finns themselves are spending increasing amounts of money on restaurants and tourist attractions such as the ski resorts of Lapland.

The State monopoly on the distribution of alcoholic beverages is now crumbling. For the time being, however, wine and spirits can only be purchased in the State-owned Alko shops. In terms of product range and quality, Alko is well prepared for competition. Most of the price on its products, however, consists of tax.

Half an island

Finland's salient characteristics from the transport point of view are its large size and low population density. With respect to the world outside, it is more than half an island.

Most of the country's imports and exports are transported by sea (the

▲ Finland has had considerable success in building luxury cruise ships. In the photo, *Enchantment of the Seas*, a cruiser built at the Kvaerner Masa-Yards' shipyard.

routes are kept open in winter by ice-breakers), although nowadays there is also a great deal of transit trade by road with Russia. Within the country, goods are transported mainly by road, while the railways specialize in heavy transports. Inland water transport routes extend from Viborg (Russia) on the Gulf of Finland to Lake Saimaa.

Foreign travellers usually arrive in Finland by air or by sea, although the country is of course connected by road to Russia and to northern Sweden and Norway. The ferries plying the Baltic Sea (Silja Line and Viking Line) are really floating hotels, frequented as much for pleasure and amusement as for getting from one country to another. There are also frequent hydro-foil connections between Helsinki and Tallinn.

Domestic air transport is well-developed. The railways have invested in state-of-the-art rolling stock, and now focus on running a few main lines and Helsinki's commuter traffic. The coach network is extensive, although many rural routes have been suppressed. The main towns are well served by public transport, but in rural areas a car is almost a must. The whole population could easily be seated in the country's two million cars. This is indeed what tends to happen at midsummer, when just about everyone leaves town for a weekend in the country.

Concentration in banking and insurance

The Finnish banking sector was deregulated in the 1980s. This emboldened the savings banks, in particular, to take such excessive risks that by the early 1990s the country found itself with a serious banking crisis on its hands. The government came to the rescue, leaving the taxpayers to foot a bill of at least 6.7 billion euro (nearly USD 10 billion at the time); the final sum will not be known until all the real estate and other security taken over by the government has been sold.

Following the bank crisis, most of the savings banks were carved up and shared out between the remaining banks. Under increasing pressure from competition, the two leading commercial banks Kansallis and the Union Bank of Finland merged in 1995 to form Merita Bank. In 1997 Merita merged with Nordbanken of Sweden, subsequently giving rise to Nordea, a joint Nordic bank. The formerly State-owned Postipankki bank has merged with the Sampo insurance company. The only remaining representative of local banking is the cooperative OKO Group. International banks, particularly Scandinavian ones, have rapidly expanded their operations in Finland.

Finnish banking is highly advanced in technical terms. Wages and salaries, for example, have long been paid direct to bank accounts. Automated teller machines are everywhere, and many families pay their bills via home computer. The office network is still shrinking as a result of increasing automation.

The insurance sector is now concentrated in the hands of three companies (Pohjola-Suomi, Sampo and Tapiola). The extensive branch of the business that handles compulsory pension insurance is largely run by private companies. The insurance and banking sectors have converged: Sampo is the first Finnish all-purpose financial institution to emerge as a result of this shift.

Banks and insurance companies have long played a key role in Finnish industry, but recently the ties have loosened. Many industries now raise funds via direct worldwide share issues; consequently, the financial institutions' hold on Finnish industry is slipping. Meanwhile, the Helsinki Stock Exchange's turnover has soared during the last twenty years. Hundreds of thousands of Finns now own shares in companies.

◀ The majority of Finns pay their bills and handle most of their other banking transactions via automatic teller or personal computer.

The world's north-ernmost farming country

Until the 1950s, agriculture was Finland's principal source of livelihood. The combination of geographical conditions and successive land reforms kept the country's farms small. Farmers supplemented their income by selling timber and doing forestry work. The number of farms has since declined to less than one quarter, or approximately 80,000. Meanwhile the average farm size has risen to almost 30 hectares. This trend is bound to continue – not least because Finnish agriculture, formerly fully protected, has been compelled by EU membership to open the doors to competition from imported goods.

Finland is the world's northernmost country in which arable farming is practicable (even in Sweden nearly all the fields are farther south). In the severe climate, yields per hectare are small by continental standards, and crops barely reach maturity just before the first night frosts arrive. Nonetheless, the Finns consider maintaining their own agricultural production a political necessity. Finland's treaty on accession to the European Union therefore allows the country to pay its farmers additional subsidies over and above the general EU support.

Animal husbandry is better suited to the Finnish climate than arable farming, although well-heated barns are a must for the winter months. Seeking new sources of income, some farmers have even started raising ostriches, which cope with the cold surprisingly well. Only some 6% of the population now live from agriculture and forestry, and many take on side jobs to supplement their income.

Although the Finns eat a fair amount of fish, fishing is not a major source of livelihood. There are many sports fishermen, however; in winter, one sometimes sees hundreds of 'ice anglers' trying their luck in the frozen lakes or coastal sea waters. The most important commercial catch is Baltic herring, while the main species fished for sport are perch and pike. Rainbow trout is being farmed in growing quantities – giving rise to criticism on account of the resulting water pollution.

▼ Animal husbandry is better suited to the climate than arable farming, although good barns are a must to provide shelter in the winter.

There are more than 200,000 reindeer in Lapland, although actually the 50,000 elk hunted yearly yield more meat. Hunting is the hobby of some 300,000 Finns. Fur farming, on the other hand, is an important though controversial source of livelihood in many rural villages.

Changing ownership structures

Finnish firms were previously owned by either families or institutions. Foreign ownership was restricted significantly until the 1990s. Some 20% of all industry was State-controlled. This was primarily in basic production, which tended to require larger capital investments than Finland's small private sector was able to provide.

Many State-owned companies have been at least partially privatized in recent years. Many of the agency-type State institutions (such as the postal service and railways) have been transformed into commercial enterprises, and efforts have also been made to stimulate competition in other areas. A number of cartels formed by private companies have been broken up.

Since the laws were amended, foreign investors have bought a large number of shares in Finnish companies. Certain firms have joined major groups of companies, particularly joint Nordic ones. On the other hand, since the 1980s Finnish firms have been purchasing many factories, even entire companies, abroad. In some cases, they have paid dear for such boldness; on the other hand, many hold that in narrowly specialized fields the only road to success is to attain international stature.

Consensus with the trade unions

The key word in Finnish economic policy has been 'consensus', meaning the tendency to seek a common understanding between businesses, trade unions, the national government and other interested parties. Consensus is no bed of roses, however, for agreements are generally preceded by lengthy negotiations, and strikes are not unusual. Generally, however, a compromise can be reached. In this system, abrupt Thatcherite reforms would be impossible; and yet, equilibrium has its value in a small country.

Some of the most important employers' organizations are *Teollisuus ja Työnantajat* (Finnish Industry and Employers, TT), *Palvelutyönantajat* (Finnish Service Employers, PT), the Central Chamber of Commerce and the regional chambers of commerce, and the Finnish Confederation of Private Entrepreneurs, which represents small businesses. The various sectors of industry naturally each have their own organization. Another influential body is the Maataloustuottajain Keskusliitto (Central Union of Agricultural Producers, MTK).

The trade unions have three different central organizations. The largest of these is the *Suomen Ammattiliittojen Keskusjärjestö* (Central Organization of Finnish Trade Unions, SAK), which comprises blue-collar workers and various junior officials and civil servants. The members of the *Suomen Teknisten Toimihenkilöjärjestöjen Keskusliitto* (Confederation of Technical Employee Organizations in Finland) are white-collar workers (including nurses), while *Akava* (Confederation of Unions for Academic Professionals) has as its members holders of academic degrees, from teachers to physicians. At 85%, the Finnish workforce's degree of organization is among the highest in the world.

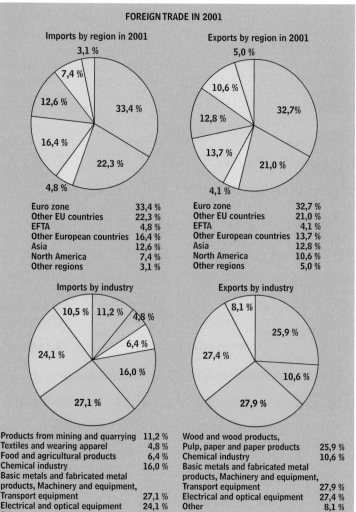

FOREIGN TRADE IN 2001

Imports by region in 2001

3,1 %
7,4 %
12,6 %
16,4 %
4,8 %
22,3 %
33,4 %

Euro zone	33,4 %
Other EU countries	22,3 %
EFTA	4,8 %
Other European countries	16,4 %
Asia	12,6 %
North America	7,4 %
Other regions	3,1 %

Exports by region in 2001

5,0 %
10,6 %
12,8 %
13,7 %
4,1 %
21,0 %
32,7 %

Euro zone	32,7 %
Other EU countries	21,0 %
EFTA	4,1 %
Other European countries	13,7 %
Asia	12,8 %
North America	10,6 %
Other regions	5,0 %

Imports by industry

10,5 % 11,2 % 4,8 %
6,4 %
24,1 %
16,0 %
27,1 %

Products from mining and quarrying	11,2 %
Textiles and wearing apparel	4,8 %
Food and agricultural products	6,4 %
Chemical industry	16,0 %
Basic metals and fabricated metal products, Machinery and equipment, Transport equipment	27,1 %
Electrical and optical equipment	24,1 %
Other	10,5 %

Exports by industry

8,1 %
25,9 %
27,4 %
10,6 %
27,9 %

Wood and wood products, Pulp, paper and paper products	25,9 %
Chemical industry	10,6 %
Basic metals and fabricated metal products, Machinery and equipment, Transport equipment	27,9 %
Electrical and optical equipment	27,4 %
Other	8,1 %

Source: National Board of Customs 2001

Recovering from depression

Finnish economic policy has changed radically over the years. True, Finland has engaged in free trade with other West European countries since the 1950s, but the Finnish economy was highly regulated and protectionist in many ways until the mid 1980s. Cor-

porate cooperation and bank-run finance groups were important; some spoke of the promised land of cartels, although the Finns hardly invented these.

We have already mentioned that the money market was liberalized rapidly during the 1980s, leading to a bank crisis. Many companies resorted indiscriminately to loans denominated in foreign currency. The collapse of

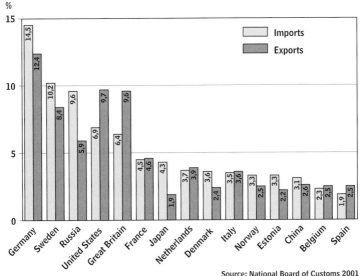

FOREIGN TRADE BY COUNTRY
Finlands main trading partners in 2001

%

Country	Imports	Exports
Germany	14,5	12,4
Sweden	10,2	8,4
Russia	9,6	5,9
United States	6,9	9,7
Great Britain	6,4	9,6
France	4,5	4,6
Japan	4,3	1,9
Netherlands	3,7	3,9
Denmark	3,6	2,4
Italy	3,5	3,6
Norway	3,3	2,5
Estonia	3,3	2,2
China	3,1	2,6
Belgium	2,3	2,5
Spain	1,9	2,5

Source: National Board of Customs 2001

FINNISH BUSINESS LEADERS

- Sari Baldauf (b. 1955), President of Nokia Networks, one of the world's leading women managers
- Aatos Erkko (b. 1932), leading publisher (Sanoma WSOY) and perhaps Finland's richest man, but something of an enigma; now approaching retirement
- Antti Herlin (b. 1956), a member of the fourth generation of a family of industrialists, is CEO of Kone, now the largest mechanical engineering group in the Nordic countries.
- Matti Honkala (b. 1945), recently appointed President and CEO of Kesko, Finland's largest retail chain
- Jukka Härmälä (b. 1946), CEO of the State-owned Finnish-Swedish Stora-Enso company
- Jere Lahti (b. 1943), outgoing general director of SOK (Finnish Co-operative Wholesale Society), a heavyweight in the coop sector
- Mikael Lilius (b. 1949), CEO of the energy conglomerate Fortum, previously a director of the Wallenberg Group in Sweden
- Juha Niemelä (b. 1946), CEO of UPM-Kymmene
- Jorma Ollila (b. 1950), chairman of the board and CEO of Nokia and architect of the company's meteoric rise
- Antti Tanskanen (b. 1946), previously a professor of economics, today general director of the group formed by the former local cooperative banks
- Vesa Vainio (b. 1942), chairman of the board of directors of the Central Chamber of Commerce
- Björn Wahlroos (b. 1952), wealthy CEO of the Sampo Group

the Soviet Union in the early 1990s did away with virtually all of Finland's government-led, bilateral 'eastern trade'. Since then, however, trade with Russia has revived – now on a private basis.

When the economy overheated in the 1980s, domestic prices soared and Finland lost some of its markets in the west. Domestic and foreign problems combined to send Finland into a deep depression in the early 1990s. At the worst time, over half a million people (about 20% of the population) were unemployed. The country has succeeded in keeping its jobless population housed and fed – indeed, according to some critics so well as to discourage the unemployed from seeking new jobs or occupations. To be sure, some people (such as small entrepreneurs who went bankrupt) genuinely had serious difficulties.

The first step to redress the situation was a 25% devaluation of the markka in 1992-93, although the exchange rate subsequently rose again. The devaluation naturally caused serious exchange rate losses to those who had taken out loans in foreign currency, but it did have the effect of reviving exports. The government resorted to heavy borrowing from abroad in order to combat the social consequences of the depression; fortunately Finland could afford this at the time.

Export growth enabled Finland to reattain the 1990 peak level of domestic product by 1995, and for many years GDP continued to grow at a brisk rate. The growth rate in 2000 reached 5.6%, but worldwide recession brought the rate down to 0.7% in 2001. Unemployment has been slow to decrease, as companies have pursued rationalization. Nonetheless, the unemployment rate has come down to well below 10 per cent, but this does not include the many people who are in training organized by the government or hold subsidized jobs.

Public sector employment also had to be cut in order to reduce government borrowing and bring taxation down a peg or two. Finland's balance of trade has been in the black since 1992, but government debt and servicing costs only began to decrease at the turn of the century. The public debt/GDP ratio is now down to 44%. Finland was ready to adopt the euro among the first group of countries to do so in 2002.

The country's economic institutions have stood up well to the test. The labour market concluded wide-ranging, moderate collective agreements several years in a row in the 1990s, and there were no major strikes during this period. The trump cards of the Finnish economy in the future will be a high standard of education, general respect of agreements, a low level of corruption and good internal security.

Scientific
Feats

For many years, Finland has been either first, second or third in the world in terms of using cellular phones, the Internet and personal computers. All through the twentieth century, while almost all other European countries have had a government monopoly on communication, Finland has had numerous private telephone companies.

Finland is also the world's major producer of cellular phones. Many of the large cruise ships sailing the high seas were built in Finland. Leading newspapers and magazines around the world are printed on paper that has been made either in Finland or with Finnish-made paper machines.

Present-day Finland is thus very much a high-tech country. Finland is also a European pioneer in information technology and liberalized tele-communication services.

From farms to factories

In 1930, about 60 per cent of the population earned their living as farmers. When World War II ended in 1945, Finland was still a relatively poor agricultural country – and farming is no easy task in the harsh northern climate. In the early sixties, about a third of the workforce was still employed in the farming sector; by 1970 their share was down to about one quarter. By then Finland was an emerging industrial society with a clear majority of the workforce in services and industry.

For many years, Finland's main exports came from its vast forests in the form of raw timber, wood products, pulp and paper. Many other industrial branches, however, were also expanding, including shipbuilding, cables, technology for the paper industry, and electronics. Industrial growth was fuelled by the steady market in the neighbouring Soviet Union.

A dramatic change has been taking place since the late 1980s. At that time the government took a deliberate decision to turn the country into a high-tech society ready for the challenges of the information age. In 1984 Finland's total research and development input was about 1 per cent of GDP, as against almost 3 per cent in the United States and Japan.

Ten years later, Finland's R&D input had already overtaken that of the US and by the year 2000 Sweden and Finland had the highest research and development input in the world. In addition to an intensified focus on R&D, the programme includes a plan to connect all Finnish schools to the Internet.

The change is reflected in the share of Finnish exports accounted by high-

▶ Well over half of Finland's inhabitants, including many schoolchildren, have a mobile phone of their own.

▶ Teamwork is the order of the day at school.

tech goods. Around 5 per cent in 1988, ten years later this figure was up to 15 per cent, and high technology thus represented the largest export segment. The value of high-tech exports first exceeded that of imports in 1995, and the gap has been widening ever since. By the end of the twentieth century, Finland was one of the most highly-developed countries of the European Union.

Education

Finland has a system of compulsory education for all children between the ages of 7 and 17. No tuition is charged. The school system ensures virtually a 100 per cent literacy rate. In the OECD Programme for International Student Assessment (PISA) in 2000, skills in reading, mathematics and scientific literacy were assessed among students of 15 years of age from 28 countries. Finnish students did extremely well: they were best in reading skills, fourth in mathematics, and third in science.

All children must attend comprehensive school for nine years. After that several avenues of further education are available, ranging from vocational school to upper secondary, followed by college and university. All stages of education – including university – are free of charge for students.

There are about twenty universities and colleges. Gaining admission is usually difficult. Entrance examinations are held in the summer, and the selection is normally based on a combination of performance at school and in the entrance exams. In addition to the formal school system, an extensive network of publicly and privately run institutes offer many opportunities for adult education.

High-tech industry in Finland

Finland's success in the sector of high technology did not appear all of a sudden from nowhere. The country has a long tradition of technological skills and training. Finland was one of the first countries in the world to set up a telephone service, and in the early days

▲ Finland has twenty universities, that of Helsinki being the biggest. The Helsinki University Library is considered to be the masterpiece of its architect Carl Ludvig Engel.

of broadcasting it had many radio and TV makers who competed successfully with foreign manufacturers. Some of these firms survived even after most of Europe's consumer electronics companies lost their markets to Asian producers.

Another contributing factor has been the Finns' high standard of education. The school system is of generally high quality. Thus it has been relatively easy for the Finnish workforce to learn to apply new technologies, and for Finnish industry to find qualified engineers. Especially since the 1990s, the universities and industry have worked in close collaboration. Much of the technological innovation is the result of this joint effort.

Pioneer technologies

Ships are not usually thought of as high-tech products, but that is exactly what modern ships are. Finland has very long traditions in shipbuilding which began in Turku in 1737 and in Helsinki in 1865. Shipbuilding was the source of many of the technical skills and traditions which would later be used in other industrial sectors. The Finnish shipyards concentrated from an early date on special-

purpose vessels, especially icebreakers. These ships required much basic research, and the shipyards developed many maritime innovations.

Many of the great cruise liners have been built in Helsinki by Kvaerner Masa-Yards. The other Finnish shipyards have continued to produce special-purpose ships, such as research vessels, tankers, offshore platforms, and vessels for oil and gas production.

Finland's first major industry was based on the country's most important natural resource, forests. It was vital for the sector to be competitive with other countries producing paper and pulp. The Finns developed special expertise in wood-processing. This expertise later became a major export item. Finland is one of the world leaders in building paper machines and designing related industrial processes. Finnish forestry expertise is applied all over the world.

An early high-tech company was Vaisala Oy, set up by Professor Vilho Väisälä in 1936 to produce a meteorological radiosonde he had developed. The company is now one of the world's leading manufacturers of electronic measurement systems for meteorology, environment, traffic

▼ **The Gulf of Finland, the Gulf of Bothnia and the Baltic Sea freeze over for many months most winters. Winter traffic in Finnish waters − and in many other northern seas − is kept going by Finnish-made icebreakers.**

safety and industrial research, exporting to more than 100 countries and with a worldwide network of distributors.

Nokia, a small town in southern Finland

In January 2000 Finland had 65 cellular phone connections per 100 inhabitants. It is no mere chance that the Finns have for many years now ranked either first or second in the world as users of cellular phones. The Helsinki-based company Oy Nokia Ab is the largest producer of cellular phones in the world.

The name Nokia is often taken to be Japanese. Who could imagine that one of the world's leading high-tech products should come from a small North European country? Nonetheless, Nokia is Finnish, and the name comes from that of a small town in southern Finland, where a small pulp mill was started back in 1865.

The company grew through expansions and mergers, becoming a wide-ranging industrial conglomerate producing paper and pulp, car tyres and rubber boots, cables, plastics and aluminium, consumer electronics and computers. An important acquisition was that of the radio and TV manufacturer Salora Oy, which provided the core facilities for the production of cellular phones, soon to be Nokia's prime asset.

Nokia came early to the cellular phone business. In the 1960s the company carried out studies of radio communications in its own laboratory. The world's first regular mobile telephone service was launched jointly by Telecom Finland and Nokia in Finland in 1972. In 1981 Nokia began to produce NMT system cellular phones in a factory next to the old Salora plant.

Ten years later Nokia entered the new GSM market as a producer of both phones and network support equipment. In the early 1990s the company took a strategic decision to concentrate on electronics and high-tech information technology products. Some of its other branches were sold off, including consumer electronics and personal computers. Today Nokia is quoted on all the major stock exchanges around the world.

The company has pioneered many new developments in the industry with products such as the pioneering Nokia 9000 Communicator, which was a combined cellular phone and palmtop computer with Internet access. Nokia and the Swedish company Ericsson jointly developed the next generation GSM cellular phone system.

Vaisala and Nokia are just two ex-

▼ Nokia's futuristic designs for third-generation mobile phone terminals.

amples of the structural changes taking place in the Finnish economy. Dozens of new high-tech ventures are born every year in the fields of information technology (both hardware and software), medical and environmental technology, industrial instrumentation, automation and system planning, as well as in biomedicine and genetic engineering. Finnish companies and research labs are also in the forefront in research on solar power cells.

Computers

For many years now, Finland has been one of the leading countries in the world in the use of computer networks and the Internet. Various explanations have been suggested, none of them conclusive. Perhaps it is easier for the taciturn Finns to communicate through a machine than by direct, face-to-face contact with unpredictable real people. This explanation seems as good as any other.

Part of the reason is that legislation on telecommunications has been liberal (by European standards). Companies, universities and individuals have been relatively free to experiment with technologies emerging from the United States. In 1987 Finland became the first European country to link up its universities to the Internet. At the same time, the general public were freely allowed to connect their computers to the telephone network to experiment with the new information technology.

▶ The Internet Café is a popular venue in downtown Helsinki. Customers can go websurfing for the price of a cup of coffee.

Nokia was one of the first European companies to make personal computers. These won praise for their ergonomic design, especially in Europe. Thus Finland's industry acquired practical experience in computer manufacturing. Nokia later sold its computer unit to the Japanese-owned company ICL.

Finland has also made some contributions on the software side of information technology. Some of the basic theories and models of computer-based neural networks were written by a Finnish professor, Teuvo Kohonen. These have found numerous applications in computer technology, from industrial processes, character recognition and robotics to methods of statistical analysis. Neural network research is in fact one of the fastest-growing areas in computer science.

Kohonen's neural networks have been used to classify galaxies discovered with the Hubble space telescope, to analyse World Bank economic data on member countries, and to find new markets for future business. Self-organizing maps (SOM) help computers recognize speech and find likely candidates for bankruptcy among investors' clients. The Internet search engine WEBSOM is also based on Kohonen's self-organizing maps.

Linus Torvalds, a young computer science student at the University of Helsinki, wanted to use the Unix operating system on his own computer. As the commercial versions of the system were too expensive, however, he set out to write his own Unix-based operating system and placed it on the Internet to be used and further developed free of charge. His challenge was well received by the Net community, and the resulting worldwide operating system Linux has become a viable competitor to Windows and Unix. Linus Torvalds joined an American company, Transmeta, and in 2000 they brought out the Crusoe portable processor, which among other things consumes less electricity.

Several software companies have entered the international market. F-Secure (formerly Data Fellows) received the prestigious European Information Technology Grand Prize in 1996 and was shortlisted in *Data Communications Magazine* in 1997 with only one other European producer as one of the Top 25 Hot Startups in its field. The company is one of the world's leading designers of anti-virus, encryption and security technology for computers, with distributors and customers practically everywhere that computers are used.

The high number of home computers is reflected in everyday life. Finns are leaders in the use of computerized home banking services. They are also increasingly making use of computer-based information services related to education, public transport, weather and entertainment.

▼ Linus Torvalds developed the Linux operating system when studying at the University of Helsinki. By 2000, Linux was the only serious competitor to Windows.

Several university departments offer open university network courses to the general public. In 1998 the Finns had the highest rate of Internet connections in the world (82 per 1,000 inhabitants), followed by Iceland (56), Norway (50), Sweden (40) and Denmark (28). The Finnish level is only matched locally in some high-tech areas of the United States.

▲ Many major Finnish companies have settled in the Keilaniemi area in Espoo, very near Helsinki. The Nokia headquarters in the foreground, followed by the offices of mobile phone operator Radiolinja, the headquarters of Kone and the energy conglomerate Fortum.

Biomedicine

Biomedicine is another of Finland's high-tech industries. An international and industrial success story is Benecol, a new type of margarine developed by the Finnish food manufacturer Raisio Oy in cooperation with Finnish medical scientists. Raisio has granted licences to the process to some of the major international food industry companies.

Finland used to have the dubious distinction of being one of the countries with the world's highest death rates due to cardiovascular disease. This was traced back partly to genetic factors and partly to the heavy traditional diet. Cardiovascular disease became a priority for medical research in Finland, which gradually amassed a great deal of internationally recognized expertise. Extensive health campaigns, such as the internationally famous North Karelia Project, have reduced the incidence of cardiovascular disease to moderate levels.

Cholesterol is necessary for health. An excessive cholesterol level in the blood, however, is one of the main risk factors for cardiovascular diseases. The Finns tend to have a significantly higher cholesterol count than people living in Southern Europe, whose diet contains less fatty foods and more fruit and vegetables.

Professor Tatu Miettinen of Helsinki University had the idea of using a harmless compound to replace some of the cholesterol in blood serum. Stanol, which is present in small quantities in all plants, turned out to be a suitable substance. Its yield, however, is small, and it is relatively expensive. Raisio Oy developed industrial methods for manufacturing stanol as a byproduct of the paper and pulp in-

dustry, and used it as an ingredient in developing Benecol. Clinical tests have confirmed that stanol significantly lowers high levels of cholesterol in blood serum. Benecol has subsequently become a commercial success.

Telecommunications

The Finnish telecommunications system is also exceptional by European standards. Most of Finland's local telephone operators have always been privately owned, and thus telecommunications have always been run as a mixed operation. There have been dozens of independent telephone companies in addition to the government-controlled company which used to form part of the Posts and Telecommunications Administration (PTT). Just as there was never any legislation to secure the government a monopoly in broadcasting, so there was never a

▲ Leena Palotie, professor of molecular biology, has studied Finnish pathogens.

▼ The new Biocenter of the University of Helsinki, located on the Viikki Campus, not far from downtown Helsinki.

▲ The northern elements are the focus of intense study. The Helsinki University of Technology (actually located in Espoo) has a cryogenics laboratory and Sodankylä a research centre that studies the Northern lights. The Arktikum science centre in Rovaniemi presents exhibitions on life in the polar regions. The centre also features sections for research, information and education.

government monopoly in telecommunications.

The government-controlled Telecom Finland changed its name to Sonera in 1998. In 2002 Sonera merged with the Swedish company Telia. The company has played an important role in developing applications of modern information technologies.

The world's coldest place?

People tend to think of Finland as a very cold country. As it is, however, the Gulf Stream keeps the Scandinavian climate relatively mild. Thus, the average temperature in Finland is considerably warmer than in American and Asian regions at similar latitudes.

Winters can be quite cold, but summers are mild and sunny. Nonetheless, for many years now Finland has held the world record for cold – in a laboratory.

The Low Temperature Laboratory of the Helsinki University of Technology is renowned for its work in low temperature physics. In the early 1970s, Professor Olli V. Lounasmaa and his research team were the first to confirm the occurrence of superfluidity in helium-3, as discovered by Nobel laureates David Lee, Robert Richardson and Douglas Osheroff.

The Finnish team developed new methods for observing helium-3 at temperatures just one thousandth of a degree above absolute zero. These observations have helped understand some of the physical processes in the very early universe, just after the Big Bang.

The work done at the laboratory has also given rise to practical applications in brain research. Professor Riitta Hari's brain research team has developed and applied a new neuromagnetic research technique called MEG. The method allows totally non-invasive studies of the brain functions of healthy individuals while awake, providing highly accurate spatial resolution and millisecond time resolution. The results have proved extremely useful for medical purposes as well as for studies in linguistics and human perception.

In addition to the studies done at the Low Temperature Laboratory, brain research has been carried out at the University of Helsinki's BioMag Laboratory. Dr Risto Ilmoniemi and his team have developed a method for magnetic stimulation of the brain. Professor Risto Näätänen has used the method to differentiate direct brain reactions to different sounds. The results have direct implications for our understanding of spoken language and of potential hearing defects in newborn babies. Näätänen's brain analysis system, called MMN (Mismatch Negativity), is now used by many laboratories around the world for scientific and clinical studies.

Finland in space?

To be sure, there are no Finnish astronauts; nor does Finland have a space programme of its own. However, as a member of the European Space Agency (ESA), the country is an active partner in space science projects.

Finnish instruments have gone into space on Russian, NASA and ESA flights. Thus, the Cassini-Huygens Probe, a joint ESA-NASA project to study Saturn and its moon Titan, carries a Finnish-made radar altimeter as well as instruments for pressure and plasma studies. Finnish scientists have also participated in the analysis of some NASA programmes. They carried out chemical analyses of some of the first moon rocks, and analysed the physiological tests made during the Columbia flight in spring 1998.

Living
in Finland

Social security

Finland is a welfare state, which means that the central government and local authorities guarantee a minimum standard of living to all citizens. Social security spending accounted for 26.7% of GDP in 1999. Although no longer among Europe's highest, this figure bears comparison with other EU countries, especially as benefits are paid primarily from tax revenues and not from private insurance schemes as in most other European countries. Care for the elderly (30%), health care (22%) and unemployment benefits (11%) account for the lion's share of social security expenditure.

The construction of Finland's present social policy began in the immediate postwar years. By 1949 welfare expenditure had risen to an average Nordic level, accounting for 10% of GDP. The real expansion of the welfare state, however, did not come until the years of economic transition in the 1960s and '70s. Whereas in the 1940s over half of the population made a living from farming, by the 1970s their proportion was down to 18% and by the 1990s to a mere 8%. Meanwhile, the number of people working in industry and in services, especially trade and communications, increased. The Finns are experts on social change and transition, having experienced abrupt transformations in occupational structure, independence, the Second World War, the resettlement of 420,000 Karelians evacuated from territory ceded to the Soviet Union following the war, and postwar reconstruction – all in the space of one century. The adaptability of the Finns was reflected most recently in the speed with which they adjusted to new technologies. There is some justification for the claim that Finland is Europe's most competitive country.

Economic growth and structural change took place in Finland in the 1960s at a rate unprecedented in European history. With the disintegration of the social safety net once provided by a predominantly rural society, new demands were made on social policy. Several reforms were undertaken in the 1960s. Old-age and disability pension systems were set up for the private sector in the early years of the decade. The most important reform in health care was the Sickness Insurance Act of 1964. The purpose of the Housing Production Act of 1966 was to stimulate the construction of housing with low-interest loans. These reforms illustrate the way the former concept of poor relief gave way to a system of social security managed jointly by the State and local authorities. The express aims of the new social policy were the welfare of all citizens and a more equitable distribution of the national income.

Finland's current social legislation covers disability due to illness or accident as well as maternity, unemployment and care of the elderly. Moreover, benefits paid include child benefits, student grants, housing allowance and child home care allowance. Individuals unable to earn a living by any other means are entitled to social assistance. Day care and various other forms of institutional care are covered by a system of social services. The public service sector has been reorganized, as local authorities increasingly complement their own service production with services purchased from the private sector.

The interesting question for both Finland and the EU as a whole is what kind of social policy model the Union will adopt in the future, and whether the social security systems of the Member States will converge as a result or whether they will retain their individual systems and forms of organization.

The family

The process of founding a family in Finland can be described as follows: a couple meets, they live together for a while, have a baby, and only then get married. This explains the statistically high percentage of unmarried couples living together, and the large number of children born out of wedlock. A typical photo in Finnish women's magazines is from the wedding of some celebrity, showing the bride and groom, and their little baby baptized at the same ceremony.

Indeed, 25% of all Finnish couples living together in 2000 were not married, when ten years earlier the figure was only 12%. The average age of marriage in 1998 was 34.3 for men and 31.7 for women, in both cases an increase of over four years since the mid 1970s. The average age of first marriage is 30.9 for men and 28.6 for women. The suggested causes of this development include changing moral standards and women's higher educational standard and career expectations.

Family size has also decreased over the last twenty years. In 1950 the average number of under 18-year-old children per family was 2.2; fifty years later it was down to 1.8. In 2000, 56,742 children were born in Finland; 29,250 were boys. The overall fertility rate (i.e. the average number of children borne by one woman) in 2000 was 1.8, and the average child-bearing age was 29.9 (for those giving birth for the first time it was 27.6). The birth rate in the 1990s differs from previous years in two respects. On the one hand, the birth rate among married and cohabiting couples is rising once more; on the other hand, the proportion of childless single women is also on the rise.

Divorces have also increased in Finland over the last twenty years. It is estimated that nearly one in four marriages end in divorce. For example,

▲ Expectant mothers are entitled to maternity grants and young mothers to parental grants. Fathers also have the option of taking paid parental leave.

29% of all marriages contracted in 1975 have ended in divorce. It is estimated that 50% of marriages contracted in 2000 will end in divorce. Finland heads European divorce statistics together with the Scandinavian countries and Britain. The growing divorce rate and the decreasing number of marriages (Figure 1) have resulted in an increasing number of single parents and families in which one or both of the parents have children from a previous relationship.

Figure 1.

Marriages contracted and divorces granted 1905–2000

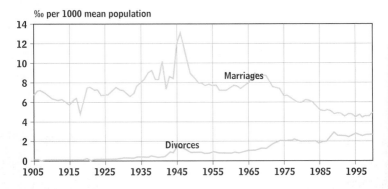

‰ per 1000 mean population

Marriages

Divorces

It is estimated that **51 percent of the marriages contracted in 2000 will end in divorce.**

Source: Statistical Yearbook of Finland 2001

The average family size in 2000 in Finland was 2.9 persons. Farmers' families are the largest, 3.4 on average, while students (1.4) and pensioners (1.5) have the lowest average (1997 statistics). The two-provider model is typical. The Finnish family thus differs from the typical Continental family in that women have an equally strong role as providers as men. Research suggests that this is due as much to finan-

▼ A family picnic in the park.
The Finnish summer is relatively short, so the Finns try to make the most of every sunny day.

▲ Following graduation exercises, divine service is held in the Cathedral for the new Ph. D.'s and M. A.'s from the Helsinki University Faculty of Philosophy.

cial necessity – in particular the high cost of housing – as to women's high standard of education and career consciousness. Rents are high and one person rarely earns enough to buy an apartment or house. Among the countries of Western Europe, Finland long ranked second to Sweden in terms of women's participation rate in the workforce, which reached almost 80% before the depression, but declined to 62% by 1999. Moreover, it is significant that compared with e.g. Sweden, women's part-time work is rare in Finland. Only 15% of Finnish women work part-time, whereas the figure in other EU countries is between 30 and 40%.

Surveys also show, however, that the younger generation (born in the 1940s or after) do not work merely for economic reasons, but also value their own individual needs, training and career. A woman's career, however, tends to come to a halt at the lower or middle echelons of the hierarchy. Statistics indicate that the formerly wide gap between men's and women's wages has narrowed.

Increasing equality has brought changes in the traditional family roles of father and mother. Here, however, there is a generation gap. Surveys show that young men participate much more frequently in household chores than their fathers did. The difference in time spent doing housework has narrowed, though it has not disappeared, over the last twenty years. According to time studies, under 35-year-old women spend some 3 1/2 hours a day and men 2 hours a day on domestic chores.

The term "new fatherhood" has been coined to describe the change in men's role. This primarily means a new relationship to children. Fathers of the younger generation spend a good deal more time with their children than the older generation did. The father is present at 70% of all childbirths, and fathers are also encouraged to accom-

▲ Sirkka Hämäläinen has made an impressive career in the predominantly male banking world: formerly Governor of the Bank of Finland, she is currently serving a five-year term on the Executive Board of the European Central Bank, which was launched in 1999.

pany the mother to prenatal and child welfare clinics more frequently than before.

Support for families with children

Mothers and families with children are supported in many ways with public funds and services. In Finland women are entitled to maternity allowance for 105 working days, 30-50 days before and the remainder after childbirth. The minimum allowance is proportional to the mother's previous level of earnings. The maternity allowance is followed by parental allowance, payable for a period of 158 days to either the mother or the father. The idea is to promote equality and to permit the mother to work at least part-time while the father looks after the baby. Few fathers have availed themselves of this opportunity, however. Fewer than half of all fathers opted for any parental allowance at all in 1996, and even those who did only took 14 days of parental leave on average. According to proposed new legislation, the father's statutory right to childbirth leave is to be extended by one week.

The most important form of family support is every child's right to day-care, for this is what makes it possible for young mothers to work. Local authorities are required by law to offer every child a place in either a day-care centre or with a family day-care provider. The latter are on the local authority's payroll. In 2000, day-care centres in Finland looked after 131,980 children, and a further 68,482 were in family day-care; local authorities thus provided day-care services for a total of over 200,000 children. Most Finns, regardless of social status or income, consider either form of day-care to be acceptable for their children. Fees vary, depending on the family's income and number of children.

Municipal day-care services are not, however, the only form of child care available. Efforts have been made during the last ten years to provide more choice for parents. Home care support is paid for child care given at home or in a private day-care centre. Families receive this benefit until the child reaches the age of three.

▲ Finnish men do their fair share of housework these days. Young fathers also spend a great deal of time with their children.

▼ The day-care centre provides children with social skills and their first friends. Statutory free meals for children are a feature unique to Finnish day-care centres and schools.

Home care support and parental allowance are both treated as taxable income. The child benefit, however, is exempt from tax. Then benefit payable for each under 17-year-old is staggered according to the number of children in the family (rising with the number of children).

Aging and social security

Finnish women had a life expectancy of 81 years and men of 74 years in 2000. Among Finland's 5.2 million inhabitants in 2000, the largest age group consisted of 50–54-year-old "baby boomers". Finland is "greying", a common trend throughout Europe (see Fig. 2). According to projections, the population will reach 5.3 million in 2020, after which it will begin to dwindle. This change will require increased public spending on the elderly, leading to a growing burden for the younger generations having to provide for them. The traditional class conflict is in fact being replaced by a generation conflict, as illustrated by the current debate on the way Finland's public debt (although not among the highest even in Europe) is being saddled on younger generations. On the other hand, the older generations defend their pension benefits, which for some are quite high, against the criticism of the young with the argument that they financed their own pensions by paying high contributions.

The pensionable age in Finland is between 60 and 65. What with early and individual retirement schemes, disability pensions and unemployment pensions, however, the average age of retirement is actually 59, unusually low by European standards. Significantly, both basic and earnings-related pension benefits are among the best in the OECD. Fully vested pension rights amounting to 60–66% of earnings can be attained with a career of from 30 to 40 years, depending on the year of birth. Owing to the generous public pension system, private schemes – which are common elsewhere in Europe – have been relatively insignificant until quite recently. The recession of the 1990s, however, boosted their popularity.

Figure 2.

Population by age and gender

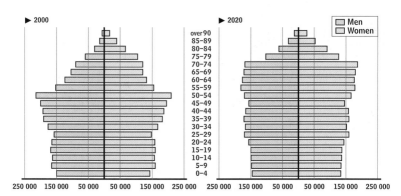

Source: Statistical Yearbook of Finland 2001

The broad scope of the welfare state is also reflected in legal provisions on the obligations of the authorities (mainly local) and the family regarding old people. The law in the Nordic countries does not recognize any other family obligations than those of parents towards their children. The legal obligation to look after one's parents was repealed in 1970. To this extent, Finland and the other Nordic countries differ from the rest of Europe. The primary responsibility of the State does not, however, mean that people neglect their parents. Studies have shown that parents in need of assistance receive 70% of the help they need from their offspring if they live in the same area.

It is unusual, however, for aging mothers or fathers to move in with their children. Old-age homes are available for elderly people unable to look after themselves. In 2000, around 9% of the over-75 population lived in such homes. In recent years, municipal and private service flats have been set up in many places, and in 2000 some 6% of the over-75s lived in such flats. Moreover, local authorities arrange domestic help for aging people. An average 30% of over-75s receive such help every week. The general policy aim is for everyone to live at home as long as she or he is capable of doing so, and to guarantee all those who must be moved to an old people's a home a room of their own and individualized care.

▼ Every effort is made to enable aging people to live at home for as long as possible. The local authorities provide nursing, home care and catering services, charged in proportion to the recipient's income. They also have the option of providing a taxi service for disabled senior citizens.

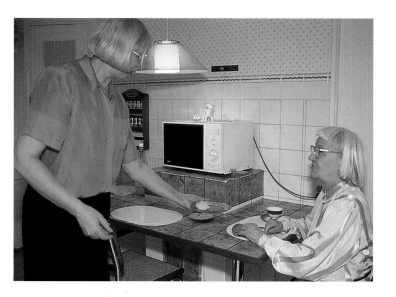

Health care and sickness insurance

The emphasis in Finnish health policy is on the availability and equitable allocation and use of services. The goal is to make public health services equally available to all, regardless of social status, income or place of residence.

Primary responsibility for providing health services rests with the local authorities. Most municipalities have at least a health centre to provide basic services. The country is divided into 21 hospital districts which provide specialized services and operate hospitals. Moreover, the universities run central hospitals which provide medical care and train physicians. Finland's health spending is average by OECD standards: in 2000 overall expenditure on health services was just over 6% of GDP and 22% of all social expenditure. The average replacement ratio provided by sickness and accident insurance (allowance per gross earnings) is just under 70% of annual income.

In terms of health indicators, Finland is one of the leading European countries. Infant mortality (i.e. deaths of under 1-year-olds) was 3.8 per thousand in 2000, lowest in the world. Prenatal care and child welfare clinics have a long history in Finland. The Mannerheim League for Child Welfare was founded back in 1920 to promote the safety of children, young people and families. Although at the time the public welfare system did not extend to child health care and protection, the League promptly set up a nationwide network of clinics providing advice and aid to expectant mothers and families with children. These clinics are now run by the local authorities.

Various forms of preventive and rehabilitative action are also available. One of the keystones of preventive health policy is cancer screening aimed at detecting the disease at an early stage. Mortality from cancer is low compared with most other countries. The results have been so encouraging that in the 1990s health policy has focused increasingly on prevention and rehabilitation.

▶ Municipal health centres provide residents with health services against a small annual fee. Many employers also offer free health services to their employees.

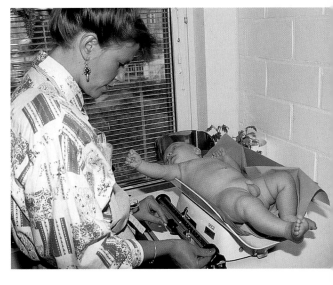

► Child health centres monitor the health and development of children closely.

Joblessness and unemployment benefits

Unemployment reached an all-time high of 18% when depression hit the Finnish economy in the early 1990s. The jobless rate had come down to 9% by the end of 2000, and according to some forecasts it should decrease further to 8% by about 2005. By the end of the 2010s, when the baby-boom generation will have retired, Finland is

▼ The unemployment rate in 2001 was around 9%. The employment offices help job-seekers find work and, if appropriate, place them in training. Self-help is still the best way to find a job, however.

expected to be suffering from a labour shortage.

Even in the peak years of unemployment, there was never the kind of unrest among the unemployed as there was in France, for example. Basic unemployment benefits and the housing allowance provide an adequate standard of living, while earnings-related benefits are relatively generous (between 60% and 66% of working income). The government has made efforts to upgrade the skills of the unemployed with adult education and other training. Under-25s must take part in some form of training in order to qualify for benefits. Many young people have had to content themselves with short-term jobs alternating with spells of unemployment.

Those who do not qualify for unemployment allowance receive social assistance. Combined with the housing allowance, this benefit amounted to roughly one third of the average Finnish wage in 2000. As in most European countries, this covers basic subsistence, or just under half the median income.

Income and taxation

Compared with the United States and many West European countries, Finland has a very even income distribution. The average monthly wage for men in 2001 was 2,354 € and for women 1,928 €. The difference is at least partly due to the fact that women and men tend to work in different fields. Disposable income of households has increased somewhat since the depression in the early '90s (Figure 3).

Taxes (at current prices) accounted for 46.2% of Finland's GDP in 2001, which was not significantly higher than in other European countries. Among West European countries, the gross tax rate was higher in Denmark and Sweden. The average income tax rate for households in Finland in 2001 was 33.3%. Surveys indicate that some 80% of the population consider the current tax rate excessive. As in other EU countries, there has been strong pressure for reducing taxation in recent years.

Figure 3.

Disposable income of households 1966–1999 (1999 prices)

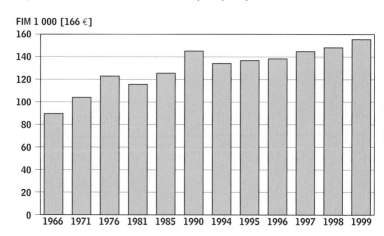

FIM 1 000 [166 €]

Source: Statistical Yearbook of Finland 2001

University graduates have higher earnings in proportion to the rest of the population than in most other industrialized countries. Nonetheless, Finland's income distribution is among the most even in the world according to OECD statistics, as progressive taxation and income transfers have an equalizing effect on earnings. Differences in net earnings, calculated using the Gini coefficient, are smaller than in France, the United States, Germany and even Sweden.

The Finnish way of life

The Finnish way of life, as expressed by standard of living, leisure habits, friendships, customs and events, has both general European aspects and distinctively Finnish features. Differences between social classes are much smaller than in, say, France or Britain. There are no salient differences in the clothes people wear; nor do their leisure occupations differ sharply according to class. Housing space, however, is clearly a function of income, and differentiates the Finns more than any other lifestyle indicator.

According to 1999 statistics, 64% of all dwellings are owner-occupied. The top income bracket live in spacious flats, row houses or single-family homes with 4 to 5 rooms on average. The average living space per person is 34.9 square metres (1999). Thus, although Finland places near the top in Europe with respect to other indicators of prosperity, the Finns' homes are small by West European standards. One of the explanations proffered for this lack of space is that the severe climate makes construction expensive. The government supports housing construction

▼ Houses in the country tend to have more living space than the often rather cramped flats in urban apartment blocks. According to an old saw, "Finns want to live in a house of their own, by a lakeside in the centre of town".

▲ The fells of Lapland are among the Finns' favourite holiday destinations. Many also regularly go cross-country skiing near their home.

by granting interest subsidies for housing loans. Moreover, many households receive a housing allowance and are granted tax deductions for mortgage interest payments. The relative increase in housing expenditure was the most conspicuous change in spending habits in the 1990s (see Fig. 4).

Figure 4.

Consumption structure of households, 1990 and 1998

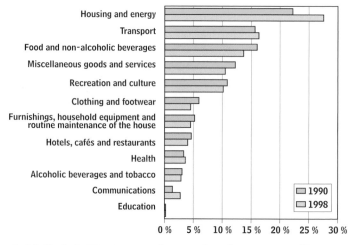

Source: Statistical Yearbook of Finland 2001   As a percentage of consumer expenditure

Differences of lifestyle in Finland in fact have more to do with a generation gap than with class divisions or income groups. As a result of the rapid postwar industrialization process, different generations have had entirely different experiences. J.P. Roos has studied the Finnish generations of the twentieth century. First came the war generation, who were born at the turn of the century. The hardships and shortages of their youth explain their ascetic, thrifty way of life. The second, the generation of postwar reconstruction and economic growth, was born in the 1920s and '30s and witnessed Finland's rapid industrialization process. This generation was characterized by entrepreneurship and a pioneer spirit.

The third generation was born during the war or just after it in the 1940s. This transitional generation experienced the rapid improvement in Finland's living standards and saw the meteoric development of technology.

This generation is still known as the baby boomers or the Bulge, as owing to the high postwar birth rate it is much larger than other age groups. According to Antti Karisto, this generation was marked by social betterment and expansion of the education system, and formed a new economic and political elite. It also differed from the previous generation in that it saw Finland's transformation from a predominantly rural culture to an urban one. Its members see themselves as the vanguard of modern society.

The younger generation are perhaps no longer united by a common background to such a degree. Many of them have no qualms about conspicuous consumption. They are individualistic youths or young adults, well versed in the new technologies, and at home in a world of mobile phones and the Internet. They tend to place a greater emphasis on social ethics than their seniors: they think people should do their work properly and

Finns tend to spend a lot of time with the family. The following statistics illustrate the average distribution of time away from work in the day of a Finn:

	Women, %	Men, %
Sleep	8.34	8.24
Household chores	3.36	2.03
TV	1.56	2.25
Physical exercise	0.29	0.39
Hobbies	0.25	0.32
Meeting friends	0.44	0.46

Source: Statistical Yearbook of Finland 2001, p. 514.

Children faithfully watch their own TV programmes and videos. Many parents also read aloud to their children.

Statistics indicate that men have more leisure time, while women spend more time on household chores.

The Finns spend an average of two hours a day watching television. TV series and entertainment programmes have the longest viewing times, followed by newscasts and sports events. Sports and exercise are indeed a crucial ingredient of Finnish culture.

expect honesty from politicians. The younger generation are clearly also more critical about society, and materialism is on the wane – paradoxical as this may seem in a consumerist era.

What do the Finns eat?

Through Swedish and Russian influence Finnish cuisine has always been international, mainly European. Domestic ingredients are often applied to new recipes. A touch of the West, another of the East, mixed with the traditions from Lapland; this is the blend that makes up the Finnish cuisine.

The Finnish culinary year

In *January* the Finns warm up with soup, roasts and casseroles. The seasonal fish is burbot, which is generally served in soup, but can also be stewed or fried. Its roe is among the most highly appreciated. Salt cured roe is served with sour cream or whipped cream, chopped onions and boiled liver, and black pepper or allspice.

On *February* 5, the anniversary of national poet Johan Ludvig Runeberg, the flags come out and everyone eats Runeberg tartlets. Shrovetide fare is also seasonal: pea soup, *blini* and special Shrovetide buns.

Easter comes in *March* or *April*. Desserts have pride of place on the table: *mämmi*, a special Finnish delicacy consecrated by the European Union, eggs filled with mouthwatering mignon chocolate, the traditional Orthodox red eggs, *pasha*, *kulitsa* and *baba* cake steeped in rum.

May is the spawning season of perch, pike, bream and Baltic herring (*silakka*), all widely available. Herring (*silli*) is *de rigueur* for May Day, as

are sweet *tippaleipä* fritters and *sima* (mead).

The summer holidays begin in *June,* when many Finns set out for the country. The new, tender shoots of rhubarb are brought in from the garden, and the first new potatoes and garden strawberries appear in shops. The whole country celebrates Midsummer with a bonfire and a sauna bath. Sausage rings and home-brewed ale or beer are on the menu. The men bring out their outdoor grills and smoke ovens for the summer.

They say the whole country shuts down in *July,* when the holiday season really gets under way. The wild strawberries, blueberries, Arctic brambles and cloudberries ripen. The "big" question of the day is whether the blueberry pie should have a shortbread crust or a leavened one. The mushroom-crazy nation picks its first ceps and chanterelles. The crayfish season begins July 21 at noon. That very night, gourmets pay a fortune for the precious crustaceans, downed to the accompaniment of vodka and drinking songs borrowed from the Swedes.

August is raspberry and currant time. The shooting season begins with pigeon, followed by duck. This is also the season for grilled lamprey, and friends compare notes at fishmongers' and market booths. Domestic pastry-cooks delight the family with apple pie.

In *September,* hunters take aim at hare and, a little later, at elk and deer. The last berries of the forest ripen: lingonberry, cranberry and, in Lapland, black crowberry. The summer homes are locked up, and the pickling season ends.

All along the west and south coast, *October* is the time of the Baltic herring market (*silakkamarkkinat*), with many festive sideshows. The islanders and fishermen bring in their autumn produce: Baltic herring prepared in every possible way, juices, breads and specialty fare. This is a harvest celebra-

▲ A medley of fish roe with sour cream and minced onions tastes delicious on *blini* or toast.

tion, rather like a muted carnival, as is the reindeer round-up in Lapland, when some of the herd is picked out for slaughter.

The hunting season ends in *November;* St. Martin's goose and "Little Christmas" parties with *glögg* (mulled wine) are the order of the day.

The big decision in *December* is whether to serve ham or turkey for the Christmas Eve dinner. The traditional accompaniments include boiled peas, prunes and casseroles made with swede, carrot or sweetened potato. These are usually preceded by a fish entrée, such as Baltic herring with various kinds of sauce, pickled herring, *gravlax* and the traditional herring salad. Prunes are served in various forms, including blancmange and 'Christmas tarts'.

▼ **Fresh-picked blueberries and milk are a special summer treat.**

What is the symbol of Finnish cuisine?

Rye bread, butter, milk and buttermilk? Potatoes? *Kalakukko* and *mämmi*? Or a certain sausage ring that the TV commercials say make the Finns happy?

In recent years, what with the flood of information, marketing, tourism and new ideas about healthy nutrition, the culinary symbols of Finland have changed. The Finns favour a light, healthy diet; they are careful about what they put in their mouths. Their motto is "eat well, feel good." In addition to their own traditional dishes, they eat "world food." Consumers are "omnivorous": they like to prepare everything from scratch, but will also settle for convenience foods on occasion. Lightness, low sodium content and low fat content are more important qualities to many than flavour. The demand for organically grown Finnish raw materials is on the rise.

The Finns appreciate fine cuisine, but consume it in moderation. Gastronomic delights and healthy habits go

hand in hand. The new millennium is expected to bring a renewed acceptance of epicureanism, a quest for gourmet experiences.

Along with the new thinking, traditional foods such as sausage are still popular. But the sausage has changed: it is meatier and tastier than ever. The animal fat in sausage is replaced nowadays with healthier vegetable fats, and enriched with ingredients that have beneficial health effects. One such additive is pine bark flour, produced in the context of a project supported by the EU.

The triumph of functional, healthful ingredients continues. The most Finnish among these is rye, which has been scientifically demonstrated to improve well-being and reduce cholesterol and the risk of coronary disease. It turns out that the Finns have in fact always had a healthy diet, thanks in part to wholemeal products (rye, barley, oats).

The researchers' list of functional products is still growing. The best-known Finnish innovation in this category has a worldwide reputation: Benecol is a cholesterol-reducing vegetable fat reputed as a remedy for all sorts of ills.

A carefully chosen, light diet

Mealtimes have changed with the times. Finnish families have many other interests besides TV. Since the hobbies of family members reduce their time together in the afternoons and evenings, the main family meal is now breakfast. It's a full meal for the Finns. Porridges are in high regard, and many families also go for muesli, bran, cereals, yoghurt and milk. Bread is a must, and the toast is increasingly of the wholemeal variety. Light margarine is a serious alternative to butter. Many households have exchanged the

▲ ▲ *Schnapps* and cheerful drinking songs are essential elements of the crayfish ritual.

▲ Salmon cooked over an open fire.

lightly roasted Finnish coffee for darker roasts, imbibed in Continental style from a glass, often as *café au lait*. Finland is a world leader in coffee consumption statistics, but tea is also gaining ground. And naturally the daily dose of vitamin C is provided in the form of juice, fruit, vegetables or berries.

Canteen meals in educational institutions and offices contain an increasing proportion of vegetables. Both schools and homes do their best to follow the recommendations of health experts, giving pride of place to grain products, potatoes and vegetables. Most of those who pack their own lunch or buy a quick snack will supplement their lunch with salads, vegetables and fruit.

Apart from water, many still drink milk, buttermilk or beer with their meals, while the small but growing group of wine-lovers have discovered to their relief that a glass or two of red wine with lunch is no longer frowned upon, even on a daily basis.

Dinner time will depend on the family members' working hours and hobbies, but the weekend is the time when most families gather around the same table. They prepare this meal together, for in many families everyone takes an interest in cooking, and baking is "in".

The cup that cheers

"It's time for a cup of coffee" is a remark you hear often in Finland. Cafés can be found in libraries, theatres, even in hairdresser's shops. Afternoon coffee is often accompanied by *pulla* buns, Danish pastries or cake. The "coffee party" is still part of most Finns' lives, but the "seven sweets" served with coffee on all festive occasions have given way to a mix between a smorgasbord and dessert buffet. Savoury tidbits, salads, sandwiches, "sandwich cake" and pasties are served along with the obligatory sweet cake or tart.

Big family celebrations are increasingly entrusted to catering services. The presentation varies from region to region, but local specialties are always prominently featured. The *karjalan-piirakka* (thin rye pasty with potato or rice filling) has been adopted over the years by the whole nation. Large quantities of this delicacy are produced industrially, but these do not hold a candle to the homemade real thing. The best *piirakka* are still fashioned by hand by Karelian matrons, baked in a traditional bread ovens and served with *munavoi*, a delicious mixture of hardboiled egg mashed with butter.

Fast food and Haute cuisine

The new age has brought rural sales outlets to many localities (generally along main roads). They offer farm-baked bread and sausage, grain products, cold meats, honey, and eggs laid by free-range hens. This is part of a new phenomenon known as culinary tourism. The old village bars have virtually disappeared, and the business of feeding travellers has been taken over by service station restaurants.

While fast food chains are spreading throughout the country, the fine restaurants keep abreast with the times. The leading chefs are well-versed in the uses of raw ingredients available in their own region, and are adept at adjusting them to Finnish tastes.

A good indicator of how well Finland is keeping up is the success of Finnish chefs in international gastronomy competitions. Fifth place in the Bocuse d'Or in Lyon is one of their more notable recent achievements. Although they may look abroad for inspiration, the self-confidence and patriotism of Finnish chefs are on the rise. They are striving to make the most of homegrown ingredients.

A chef preparing a representative Finnish buffet might select the following delicacies: fish roe with accompaniments, *gravlax* or smoked fish, smoked ham or lamb, soft white cheese, beetroot-carrot-herring salad and Finnish vegetables, and dark rye

▲ Coffee time.

bread. The main course might be fish from one of the thousands of lakes or prime beef or game, served with wild mushrooms, potatoes and fresh vegetables free from chemical residues. All this is followed up with a selection of Finnish cheese and, for dessert, fresh berries from the forest or garden, topped with a dollop of ice cream.

The final touch is provided by coffee and a glass of one of Finland's exquisite berry liqueurs.

Sports

Finland's countryside is unspoilt, an irresistible invitation to get up and go. Running, skiing, swimming, rowing, canoeing, orienteering and cycling are popular sports, combining the joy of physical exertion with the great outdoors. There are also numerous indoor sports complexes to choose from.

The most popular forms of outdoor recreation include walking, cycling, cross-country skiing and swimming. Among team sports, 'floorball' has won a large following over the last ten years or so. The classic team sports are (European) football in summer and ice hockey in winter. Finland's national sport *pesäpallo*, is a variety of American baseball, a favourite summer sport especially in rural areas and in the smaller towns. Recent additions to the repertoire include snowboarding in winter, rollerblade, rollerboard and 'Nordic walking' (supported by poles) in the summer.

Many mass events are held in Finland. A traditional one is the *Jukolan viesti*, an all-night orienteering relay, accompanied by the *Venlojen viesti*, a similar event for women's teams. For two days, thousands of contestants camp out near the starting area, where things sometimes get as crowded as at a rock festival. A rather different event is the Helsinki Cup, a soccer jamboree for young players that attracts over 800 teams from around the world. Thousands of Finns take part in the biggest cross-country skiing event, the 75-kilometre Finlandia race. Most of the competitors are there just to enjoy the exercise and companionship, but it's serious business for the top contenders. The annual Helsinki City Marathon in August also attracts thousands of participants.

The crucial moment in the history of Finnish competitive sports came during the 1912 Olympic Games in Stockholm. Nationalist feeling ran high at the time, and the movement for independence from Russia was gaining momentum. An inkling of things to come was provided by the opening ceremony, where the Finnish team marched behind its own name-board, separate from the Russian team. The games themselves were a huge success for Finland, which won nine gold medals. Hannes Kolehmainen, the first "Flying Finn", became the national hero by winning the 5000 and 10 000 metres and the cross-country race. Kolehmainen was succeeded in this role by Paavo Nurmi, the all-time champion of long-distance running. Nurmi won nine gold and three silver medals during his career, one of the greatest achievements in Olympic history.

The most successful athletics events for Finland have been long-distance running and javelin throwing. The javelin, in particular, has been dominated by Finns, who have won nine Olympic gold medals and numerous world championships and European championships in the event. The first major success came in 1912 in Stockholm, where the Finnish javelin team led by Julius Saaristo took all three medals. The most recent major gold medal in the event went to Heli Rantanen, who won the women's javelin in the 1996 Olympic Games in Atlanta. The Finns have been less successful in running in recent years. The last "Flying Finn" was Lasse Virén, who won both the 5000 and the

10 000 metres in the 1972 and 1976 Olympic Games. No other runner has ever taken the long-distance "double" in two consecutive Olympics.

Finns have also had a great deal of success in many contests of strength. They dominated the international wrestling scene in the early 20th century, having easily the best team in 1912 and at all the Olympics in the 1920s. Such feats are no longer possible, but the Finnish Greco-Roman wrestlers are still among the international elite. The great Finnish name in weightlifting was Kaarlo Kangasniemi, who won gold in the world championships, European championships and Olympics in the late 1960s and early '70s.

The Finns have never done so well in summer team events. They have, however, taken great strides in the "royal game", football, over the last ten years or so. Many Finnish players have been recruited by European professional teams, and have had no small success. For some years now, the brightest Finnish stars in the sport have been Jari Litmanen, who has played for Barcelona, Liverpool, and Ajax Amsterdam, and Liverpool's star defender Sami Hyypiä.

The first Finnish world championship golds in swimming went to Antti Kasvio in the 200 metres freestyle and to Jani Sievinen in the 200 metres medley in 1994. Sievinen also won Olympic silver in the same event in 1996, and has set a dozen world records over the years.

The Finns have done well in many winter sports. One of the early heroes was the speed skater Clas Thunberg, also known as "the Nurmi of the ice rink." He won a total of five golds, one silver and one bronze in Olympics, and was crowned champion of the world and of Europe many times over. Petri Kokko and Susanna Rahkamo won gold in the European championships and silver in the world

▲ Finland's best footballer Jari Litmanen, here in the blue-and-white colours of the national team.

▼ The Sulkava rowing regatta attracts almost 10 000 participants every July.

► Finland has a tradition of success in motor racing. Kimi Räikkönen is one of the rising stars on the Formula One circuit.

championships in ice dancing in 1995.

Finland has had many heroes in Nordic skiing. The first Olympic winner was Veli Saarinen, who took gold in the men's 50 kilometres in 1932. Veikko Hakulinen was the big star in the 1950s. Eero Mäntyranta succeeded him in the '60s, winning the relay gold in the 1960 Olympics and two golds and a silver in 1964. The best athlete overall at the 1984 Winter Olympics in Sarajevo was Marja-Liisa Kirvesniemi, who won three gold medals – all the women's individual events. The Finnish Olympic winner in 1988 was Marjo Matikainen, today known as a member of the European Parliament, and in 1992 it was Marjut Lukkarinen's turn to win. Among the men, one of the most successful skiers of the last few years is Samppa Lajunen, who won gold in all three Nordic combined events in the Salt Lake City Olympic Games in 2002.

► Samppa Lajunen crosses the finishing line to take gold for Finland in the 4x5 km Nordic combined relay in the Salt Lake City Winter Olympics 2002.

The Finns have been equally successful, if not more so, in ski jumping.The first Finnish Olympic champion in this discipline was Antti Hyvärinen in 1956, and since him Finns have frequently topped major events. The greatest ski jumper of all time was Matti Nykänen, who won four Olympic golds and five world championships in the 1980s. After Nykänen, the biggest names have been Toni Nieminen, who took two golds and one bronze in the 1992 Olympics; Ari-Pekka Nikkola, on the podium time and again in the team event; Jani Soininen, who won gold and silver in Nagano in 1998, and Janne Ahonen, world champion in 1997. Finland took silver in the Olympic team event in 2002.

The first Finnish world championship in Alpine skiing went to Kalle Palander in the slalom event in 1999. A number of Finns are leading contenders in one of the most popular new winter events, snowboarding. Janne Lahtela took gold in the moguls in the Salt Lake City games.

The most popular winter event of all in Finland, however, is ice hockey. The Finnish team had fairly mediocre results until 1988, when Finland took the silver medal in Calgary. The next major success came in 1992, when Finland played in the World Championship finals, though it lost to Sweden. At last in 1995, the roles were reversed. The best-known Finnish hockey players are Jari Kurri and Teemu Selänne. Kurri is in fact the most successful European player of all time in the National Hockey League, while Selänne, also known as "The Finnish Flash", has been the NHL's highest-scoring player twice.

Today's biggest Finnish stars, however, are racing drivers. Two Finns have won the most prestigious racing series of all, Formula One: Keijo ("Keke") Rosberg, crowned world champion in 1982, and Mika Häkkinen, who took the crown in 1998 and 1999.

There have been many champion rally drivers from Finland. The first to become world champion was Ari Vatanen in 1981. Juha Kankkunen won the world championship no less than four times in the 1980s and '90s. This feat was equalled by Tommi Mäkinen, who won the championship four times running from 1996 to 1999. Marcus Grönholm was world champion in 2000 and 2002.

Culture

The Finns have a special respect for culture. J.V. Snellman, a 19th century statesman and the leading Finnish philosopher, wrote that a small nation's power was in its culture; it was the only means to advancement. Though a Swedish-speaker himself, Snellman was an enthusiastic propagator of the Finnish language and literature. His grand idea was the making of a unified Finnish nation; and made it was. The idea of national education spread across the social spectrum, down to the lowliest peasant. Even today, culture enjoys significant government support, the most striking results being seen in the field of music.

Architecture

Even today, Finland is a country of modern architecture. In the old days, most buildings were made of wood, which is not as durable as stone. What is more, for centuries Finland served as a battleground, and some wars laid waste to virtually the whole country. Thus no less than 90% of all buildings date from the period of independence, i.e. from after 1917. And the homes of one third of all Finns were built less than twenty years ago.

All the same, a number of precious historical monuments have survived. There are over seventy handsome mediaeval greystone churches, the oldest of them in Åland, near Turku and along the south coast. True, there has been some controversy of late about the age of these buildings, and it now seems as if several churches previously thought to date from the 13th century were actually built a hundred years later or so.

A few wooden churches from the 17th century have been preserved, notably at Petäjävesi, Paltamo and Keuruu. An unusual sight is Kerimäki Church, one of the world's largest wooden structures, big enough to seat a congregation of 4,000. Built in 1849, this shrine also hosts many well-attended concerts in summer.

◀ The mighty walls of Olavinlinna Castle provide a magnificent setting for the summer opera festival in Savonlinna.

Another interesting chapter in Finnish history is recalled by a handful of mediaeval stone castles. No trumpets of war sound from their walls today; instead, the beautifully restored castles of Turku, Häme and Olavinlinna (the home of the annual Savonlinna Opera Festival), are now dedicated to cultural pursuits.

The splendidly romantic island fortress of Suomenlinna (or Viapori) lies off the coast of Helsinki, just a short boat trip away. The "Gibraltar of the North", built by Augustin Ehrensvärd (1710–1772), this was the largest construction project of its time in Scandinavia; today it is a historic site renowned throughout Europe and a UNESCO World Heritage Site.

Only a small number of historic homes have been preserved, although several small towns still have whole districts of wooden houses, an unusual sight in Europe. Also worth seeing are the industrial estates of the seventeenth century, the major tourist draws being Fiskars, Mustio and Ruotsinpyhtää on the south coast.

▲ Senate Square, designed by Carl Ludvig Engel in the early 19ᵀᴴ century, still serves its original purpose perfectly today. Left to right, the University, the University Library, the Cathedral and, in the foreground, the Palace of the Council of State. The four small corner towers are of later date.

The rural Empire style of the early nineteenth century is represented notably by churches, parsonages and wooden manor houses, many of them designed by the German-born architect Carl Ludvig Engel (1776–1840). Helsinki owes a particular debt of gratitude to Engel for the fine Empire buildings fringing Senate Square: the cathedral, university, Council of State and many smaller buildings form one of Europe's most unified Neoclassical architectural settings. On the other hand, Engel can be grateful to Helsinki, for few architects in the world ever had the chance to design a whole new capital city. This, however, is exactly what Engel was ordered to do in the early 1800s by decree of the Russian Tsar.

◀ The Sibelius Hall in Lahti is a sample of contemporary Finnish architecture. Designed by Hannu Tikka and Kimmo Lintula, this combined congress centre and concert hall is the largest wooden building erected in Finland in the last 100 years.

Finland's fame as a forerunner in modern architecture dates from the rise of the Art Nouveau movement (called National Romanticism or Jugend in Finland) around 1900. The forward-looking nation, defying Russian efforts at assimilation, was a hotbed for new ideas. Finns deliberately strove to establish a distinctive national culture, collecting funds for many new public buildings in a show of independence.

▶ The dining room is one of the most charming interiors in the Villa Hvitträsk. The sofa in the window niche is covered by a richly decorated weave designed by Eliel Saarinen. A lovely view of the shimmering lake below opens up from the window.

▶ Architects Raili and Reima Pietilä provided an object lesson on the potential of concrete for creating free forms in Dipoli, the Helsinki University of Technology student union building. The irregularly shaped segments of the building rise straight out of the rock.

ALVAR AALTO

■ The surprise winner of an architectural competition held for the Viipuri Library in the mid 1920s was a young, little-known architect by the name of Alvar Aalto (1898–1976). His winning design, a bold, airy combination of wood, concrete, glass and brick, was something completely new; perhaps even more surprisingly, it was carried out virtually unmodified. After the city of Viipuri was taken over by the Soviet Union following the Second World War, the library was abandoned for many years and suffered serious damage.

Aalto's next competition victory, the Paimio Sanatorium, was built between 1929 and 1933, and is another landmark in the history of modern architecture. With his architect wife Aino, Aalto worked out every detail of the building, down to the reclining chairs, light fixtures and wash-basins, to perfection.

A remarkable use of light, harmony with the natural surroundings, curving forms, an unusual treatment of wood and youthful optimism characterize all of Aalto's buildings, from the Villa Mairea, a private residence (1938) in Noormarkku, to Säynätsalo Town Hall (1952), Jyväskylä University (1952–57) and the town centre of Seinäjoki (1960–87).

◀ The Villa Mairea is an L-shaped house designed by Alvar Aalto. The main floor was designed for receiving guests and the upper floor for family life. The garden features a sauna and a swimming pool of irregular shape.

The Finnish pavilion at the World Fair in Paris in 1900, designed by the trio Armas Lindgren (1874–1929), Herman Gesellius (1874–1916) and Eliel Saarinen (1873–1950), triggered a downright furore for Finland in Europe at the turn of the century. The Villa Hvitträsk, built by the three architects near Helsinki, was the supreme achievement of the Jugend movement, embodying its ideals of comfort, freedom and affinity with nature.

Hardly any other city in the world has preserved its Art Nouveau quarters as intact as the Katajanokka district, the stronghold of National Romanticism in Helsinki. Another prime example of the style is Tampere Cathedral, designed by Lars Sonck (1870–1956).

The Functionalist movement was also taken very seriously by the Finns in the 1920s and '30s. Alvar Aalto (1898–1976) and Erik Bryggman (1891–1955) strove for a natural lifestyle based on the three cornerstones of reason, light and healthfulness. Bryggman's Chapel of the Resurrection in Turku is drawn with a delicate touch and makes sophisticated use of natural light; together with the Åbo Academy library, it represents Finnish Functionalist architecture at its finest.

The third golden age of Finnish architecture came in the 1950s, with Aulis Blomstedt (1906–1979) and Viljo Revell (1910–1964) among the pioneers of the new idiom. Rising from the shadows of war, Finland went through a period of reconstruction, industrialization and urbanization. New churches, schools, libraries, town halls and apartment blocks sprang up everywhere. Green suburbs were built, the "garden town" of Tapiola in Espoo showing the way. Unfortunately, the Modernist fever led to the needless destruction of much that was old and valuable.

Luminosity and light forms are still the key to Finnish architecture today, characterizing the works of architects such as Kristian Gullichsen (b. 1932) and Juha Leiviskä (b. 1936). In the buildings of Reima Pietilä (1923–1993) and Raili Pietilä (b. 1926), such as the *Dipoli* students' centre and the Tampere Library, known as the *Capercaillie*, Classical harmony gives way to caprice and surprise. The Finnish Embassy in Berlin, designed by three young architects Rauno Lehtinen, Pekka Mäki and Toni Peltola, was named the world's "best building of the year" in 2001. Meanwhile, old building methods, such as wood construction, are gradually coming into their own again, although traditionalism all too often takes the form of Postmodern quotations. Finland is still the promised land of Modernism.

Design

Finnish design was a household word in the 1950s and '60s. At the Milan Triennale in 1951, the year of the great breakthrough, Finnish designers won six Grand Prix, seven gold medals, eight silver medals and four honourable mentions. At the next few events, Finns took one quarter of all the awards on offer. Suddenly the names of Gunnel Nyman (1909–1948), Kaj Franck (1911–1989), Tapio Wirkkala (1915–1985) and Timo Sarpaneva (b. 1926) were on everybody's lips.

The new design idiom became the symbol of a new beginning for Finland, as the country emerged from the trauma of war and the dreary years of reconstruction. There was strong demand for modern utility objects. Finns had maintained strong emotional ties with their rural heritage, to which they returned in seeking renewed simplicity. Bridging the gulf between the traditional and the modern, designers combined the best of both, turning their back for good on the ostentation of the years between the wars.

Finnish designers also embraced the originally Swedish idea of "more beautiful everyday objects", giving pride of place to natural materials and uncomplicated forms. Louis Sparre (1863–1964) and other Art Nouveau designers at the turn of the century had devised a new look for furniture and ceramics, seeking inspiration in the traditional form of the *Kalevala* country, particularly East Karelia. This tradition is carried on today by the popular jewellery firm *Kalevala-koru*.

An even more influential model for the new generation of the '50s was Alvar Aalto, the leading architect of the organic Functionalist movement, who also designed most of the interiors of his buildings, including furniture and light fixtures. The interior decoration company Artek, founded by Aalto in 1935, initially concentrated on marketing Aalto's own designs. Some of its international classics were birch chairs and tables with legs made of bent plywood and the beautifully shaped, wavy Savoy vase.

Marimekko, a garment and fabric store founded by Armi Ratia (1912–79), revolutionized the traditional ideas of good taste and correct colours. A spate of young, boldly experimental designers, including Maija Isola (b. 1927) and Vuokko Eskolin-Nurmesniemi (b. 1930), produced colourful but clean-lined fabrics and clothes which sealed Marimekko's international success.

Finnish utility ware took on a whole new look. Even the most ordinary Finnish home filled up with new design articles: glasses, vases, textiles, pots and pans, scissors and other objects which elsewhere represented rarefied elitism. Especially the ergonomically designed, orange-handled Fiskars scissors have been a fixture in every Finnish home since the 1960s. They are said to be the world's most plagiarized product.

In the 1950s Finland was like one great building site, and modern design provided the perfect match for the architecture of the new buildings. The design revolution also reflected more general social changes: a streamlined vase or a curtain with bold colours and patterns served to express their

▶ The "Chanterelle" vase by **Tapio Wirkkala**.

▶ The Marimekko collection still features the stripes that made the company famous, although designers have changed over the years. The shirts in the photo were designed by Annika Rimala.

owners' new, more liberal attitudes.

Industry, too, contributed to the change, shifting the focus from expensive, unique *objets d'art* to serially produced and moderately priced utility objects.

The young generation has taken up the challenge of this recent past, cultivating a more relaxed attitude to tradition along with the now familiar, polished modernist idiom, and experimenting with an increasing range of natural and recycled materials.

Paper art made a rather late appearance in Finland, but when it was taken up, the results were impressive. One of the leaders in the field is Janna Syväoja (b. 1960); like many other designers of her generation, she uses recycled paper to make elegant jewellery and other ornamental objects.

▼ Three brooches with animal motifs by Kalevala-Koru.

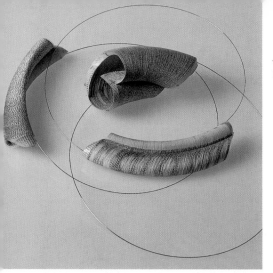

Art

Finnish art has been highly successful in merging national and international influences. The various isms have taken on a distinctly Finnish garb here, adapted to the local mentality, landscape and climate. Even the severest abstract modernism is imbued with the warmth of natural forms, as seen in the flowing lines of the sculptures of Kain Tapper (b. 1930) and others, reflecting the smooth surface of the Finnish bedrock.

The first Finnish painter to rise to European standard was Werner Holmberg (1830–1860), who studied in Dusseldorf in the 1850s. Before his time, the gentry commissioned their portraits from itinerant painters known as "counterfeiters," most of whom were of foreign origin. One of the best Finnish painters among them was Margareta Capsia (1682–1759), Finland's first woman artist. Mikael Toppelius (1734–1821) was a prolific religious painter who filled many churches in northern Finland with didactic religious imagery.

The Finnish artists of the late nineteenth century flocked to the studios of Paris, bringing back the fashions of outdoor painting and impressionism when they returned. The new continental style of painting, however, presented an almost insuperable challenge back in the home country: how to capture on canvas the cool, translucent northern light; the midnight sun in summer; the cold, glittering, blue lakes; the brooding forest, with spruce trees standing to attention in military fashion; the snow and ice with their endless shades of white? These were the problems tackled by painters such as Albert Edelfelt (1845–1905), highly successful in the salons of Paris and a precursor of impressionism in Finland, who also depicted the Finnish country people in images of idealized dignity.

The National Romantic and Symbolist movements of the turn of the century gave rise to the "golden age" of Finnish art. Akseli Gallen-Kallela (1865–1931) created an imagery from the *Kalevala* which is still part of the national identity. The drawings and watercolours of Hugo Simberg (1873–1917), Gallen-Kallela's pupil and protégé, are highly prized today. Simberg translated Finnish folk tales into a fairytale world of his own, peopled with little devils and wounded angels.

▶ The painting *The Wounded Angel* by Hugo Simberg in Tampere Cathedral.

▶ Akseli Gallen-Kallela's painting *Kullervo's Curse*.

◄ *The Seamstress* by Helene Schjerfbeck.

Women painters made their mark early in Finland. Fanny Churberg (1845–1892) was a bold stylist and colourist who paved the way for her younger colleagues, such as Maria Wiik (1853–1928) and Helene Schjerfbeck (1862–1945).

The Parisian-style naturalism introduced in Finland by Schjerfbeck and her "sister painters" aroused considerable controversy at the time. Over the years, Schjerfbeck developed into a highly individualistic, elegant modernist, whose work began to gain the international attention it deserves only towards the end of the twentieth century.

The role of women in Finnish art has continued to grow. Today's pioneers, such as Marita Liulia (b. 1957), Eija-Liisa Ahtila (b. 1959) and Henrietta Lehtonen (b. 1965), work with new media, including CD-ROM and video art.

Postwar Finnish art has been marked by a debate between Constructivism and Expressionism, intellectual control and emotional extravagance. The precise, carefully planned forms of Sam Vanni (1908–93), Juhana Blomstedt (b. 1937) and Matti Kujasalo (b. 1945) contrast with a pitiless dissection of emotions in the works of Aimo Kanerva (1909–91), Marika Mäkelä (b. 1947) and Marjatta Tapiola (b. 1951).

Today's young generation prefers to maintain an ironic distance from the archetypal Finnish images. A frequently seen guest at the international forums of the '90s was Esko Männikkö (b. 1959), a photographer specializing in portraits of humble northern folk – particularly lonely backwoodsmen – and a virtuoso treatment of atmosphere reminiscent of Vermeer.

Notable Finnish artworks can also be found outside galleries and museums. Although many of the wall paintings in the mediaeval greystone churches were hidden behind a coat of whitewash in the days of the Lutheran Reformation, some remarkably evocative frescoes from the early sixteenth century have been preserved, notably in the churches of Hattula, Lohja and Rymättylä. The colourful figures of saints in ancient altar screens were also destroyed after the Reformation, with the result that the interiors of most Finnish churches are extremely ascetic.

The country's oldest artworks,

however, are rock paintings dating from between 3000 B.C. to the beginning of the Christian Era. They mostly depict game – elk, deer and bear – hunted and worshipped by the nomadic tribes of the north. The same motifs can be found in ritual objects, the finest of which are genuine works of art.

Music

Every now and then people ask how it is possible that a country the size of Finland can keep producing so many top-notch conductors, singers and musicians.

The answer is simple: Finland has a decentralized system of music institutes offering basic musical education around the country, even in small towns. The 150 institutes in the network, from north to south, sift out the country's musical talent most effectively.

The early history of Finnish music has little to boast about. There was no royal court, and therefore no court orchestra. Art music was generally confined to the manors and parsonages:

SIBELIUS

■ Jean Sibelius (1865–1957) was hailed in his day not only as a musical genius, but as the champion of a nation struggling for its independence.

He handled his PR job with aplomb. Seven symphonies, a violin concerto, *Finlandia* and *Valse triste* proclaimed the plight of the composer's native country around the world. *Kullervo*, *Karelia* and *Tapiola* were unabashedly patriotic works. Thus Sibelius's music came to be seen as representing northern emotions and nature.

Sibelius has always been well-loved in Finland and the Anglo-Saxon world. In recent years his music has also been gaining ground in France and Germany. Osmo Vänskä and the Lahti Symphony Orchestra have been showered with international awards for their renderings of the Sibelius Violin Concerto, *The Tempest*, *En saga* and the recently rediscovered tone poem *Skogsrået* (The Wood Nymph).

One of the leading performers of the Sibelius Violin Concerto is Pekka Kuusisto. In 1995, at the age of 19, he became the first Finn to win the International Sibelius Violin Competition, a prestigious event held only once every five years.

△ *Portrait of Jean Sibelius* by Akseli Gallen-Kallela.

WORLD STARS

■ There are surprisingly many Finns among the top conductors on the international circuit. Esa-Pekka Salonen (b. 1958), Jukka-Pekka Saraste (b. 1956), Sakari Oramo (b. 1965), Osmo Vänskä (b. 1953) and Juha Kangas (b. 1945) take turns conducting the world's leading orchestras and their home troops in Finland. The youngest virtuoso is Mikko Franck (b. 1980). The Sibelius recordings of Osmo Vänskä and the Lahti Sinfonietta have won a series of international awards.

There are also many internationally acclaimed Finnish opera singers. The German opera houses alone have some forty Finnish singers on their payroll. Matti Salminen (b. 1945), Jorma Hynninen (b. 1941), Soile Isokoski (b. 1957), Karita Mattila (b. 1960) and Monica Groop (b. 1958) are stars who appear regularly in the major opera houses of the world.

Pianists Ralf Gothoni (b. 1946) and Olli Mustonen (b. 1967) and cellists Arto Noras (b. 1942) and Jan-Erik Gustafsson (b. 1970) are among the numerous Finnish musicians who have forged an international career for themselves. Finland's leading orchestras include the Radio Symphony Orchestra (Helsinki), the Helsinki Philharmonic, the Tapiola Sinfonietta, and the Central Ostrobothnian Chamber Orchestra (Kokkola).

▲ Esa-Pekka Salonen.

▲ Jukka-Pekka Saraste.

▲ Osmo Vänskä.

▶ Kaija Saariaho ranks among the world's leading contemporary composers.

▲ Apocalyptica. Infernal-symphonic heavy metal salvos on the cello.

the lowlier rural population sang, at home and in church, sometimes in four-part harmony if the church had no organ.

The music of Bernhard Henrik Crusell (1775–1838), the "Northern Mozart", is still frequently played, but it was only with the emergence of Jean Sibelius (1865–1957) that Finnish music became more widely known.

The towering figure of Sibelius overshadowed his many talented contemporaries. The modernist opera *Juha* (1922) by Aarre Merikanto (1893–1958) was rediscovered only after decades of oblivion. Recently the works of Leevi Madetoja (1887–1947) and Erkki Melartin (1876–1937) have also enjoyed something of a revival.

Present-day Finnish composers go their own ways. Einojuhani Rautavaara (b. 1928), Kaija Saariaho (b. 1952) and Magnus Lindberg (b. 1958) are among those who have gained world fame. A special success story is that of contemporary Finnish opera. Recent works to win acclaim include *Kullervo*, based on a theme from the *Kalevala*, and *King Lear*, both by Aulis Sallinen (b. 1935), and Saariaho's *L'amour de loin*.

Two of the best-known Finnish folk groups are Värttinä and Angelin

SUMMER IS FESTIVAL TIME

■ The traditional, sleepy lakeside cottage holiday gave way in the 1960s and '70s to the bustle of summer music festivals, with opera in Savonlinna, folk music in Kaustinen, chamber music in Kuhmo, Naantali and Mustasaari, new music in Viitasaari, organ music in Lahti, rock in Ruissalo, tango in Seinäjoki and jazz in Pori.

The combined attendance for all Finnish summer festivals is well over a million. Audiences are mostly Finnish, but the number of foreign visitors is growing, as the Savonlinna Opera Festival and the Kuhmo Chamber Music Festival, in particular, are widely considered to rank among the outstanding events in the world in their categories.

tytöt, whose brand of world music has won international success. The leading young jazz musicians include Trio Töykeät, Antti Sarpila Swing Band, sax player Jukka Perko, vibraphonist Severi Pyysalo, pianist Lenni-Kalle Taipale and U-Street All Stars. Apocalyptica, a group of young musicians from the Sibelius Academy, plays heavy rock, but also resorts on occasion to a more melodious vein.

Dance

In 1921 Finland's cultural scene was abuzz: the founding of a national ballet as an extension of the Finnish Opera made the newly independent republic fully autonomous also in artistic terms.

The ballet's opening performance was *Swan Lake* – no surprise, considering that the whole project was the brainchild of Edvard Fazer

(1861–1943), a former impresario of the Russian Ballet. Russia had already provided neighbourly encouragement before: the visits of St Petersburg's Mariinsky Theatre, in particular, had been hugely successful.

Meanwhile, new winds in the dance world were blowing from the West. Isadora Duncan enthralled her audience at the Finnish National Theatre in 1905. Inspired by Duncan's performance, Maggie Gripenberg (1881–1976) founded a free dance group which eventually gained international fame with her Sibelius choreographies.

The general public cared little for the aestheticism of art dance. Only a handful of enthusiasts attended the performances of the much-vaunted modernists of the 1950s. The young radicals of the '60s, however, finally discovered the roots of the nation in dance. The free dance group Raatikko translated the classics of socially com-

TANGO

■ As soon as the wartime ban on dancing was lifted, open-air summer dancing began to spread like wildfire in Finland. Platforms were set up in the green countryside, where waltzes and foxtrots resounded. The undisputed favourite, however, was the tango,

▼ The Finns adore the tango.
The Tango Festival in Seinäjoki.

which captured the emotional essence of the Finns, ranging from silent longing to blazing passion.

Tango buffs have had their own festival in Seinäjoki since 1985, with concerts, dances and contests regularly drawing over a hundred thousand aficionados.

The Finnish tango king Eino Grön (b. 1939) now has a crown prince in Jari Sillanpää (b. 1965), while thousands of aspiring hopefuls practice in the hundreds of karaoke bars that have sprung up around the country.

"Ladies' choice" is among the liveliest phenomena in Finnish popular culture. The purpose of the exercise is strictly confined to dancing. The ladies are of an independent ilk, so a gentleman who finds himself at such an event should not be alarmed if asked by a most respectable matron for the honour of a tango.

mitted literature all the way back to Aleksis Kivi's seminal *Seven Brothers* (1980) into the language of dance. They also recycled the Icelandic writer Halldór Laxness's novel *Salka Valka*.

Ever since then, Finnish dance groups have sought to break with tradition or to reinterpret it, now turning the national epic, the *Kalevala*, into a comedy of manners, now projecting the *Kanteletar*, a collection of lyrical folk poetry, as a pageant of masculine bluster and feminine melancholy.

The high-water mark of Finnish dance came in the 1980s. The psychological dance dramas of Jorma Uotinen (b. 1950), such as *Forgotten Horizon* (1980) and *The Shout* (1985), initially met with bewilderment, then gradually with growing appreciation. Uotinen, who had been a member of Carolyn Carlson's group at the Paris Opera, was appointed head of the Helsinki City Theatre dance group in 1980. He went on to direct the National Ballet from 1991 to 2001.

A new, urban energy suffuses the work of Kenneth Kvarnström (b. 1963) and his dance group, while Ari Tenhula (b. 1964) makes use of the idiom of Japanese Buto, Arja Raatikainen (b. 1958) of shamanism and Tero Saarinen (b. 1964) of the theatre of the absurd and silent film. Sanna Kekäläinen (b. 1962) and Kirsi Monni (b. 1963) explore the perspective of modern women.

The Finnish dance scene converges in June on the town of Kuopio, in the midst of the Finnish lakeland. The Kuopio Dance and Music Festival provides a classy but informal annual overview of the state of the art.

The Kaustinen Folk Music Festival in July attracts over one hundred thousand tradition buffs yearly. New folk dance is no mere dainty tripping; it has an earthy, often downright boisterous quality about it.

Theatre

A veritable theatre fever possessed the Finns in the nineteenth century: every local club and association, even in the smallest of communities, had its own theatre performances and poetry recitals, or at least arranged visits to theatres in the towns. The first playhouses were built in Viipuri, Turku and Helsinki around the year 1800; soon amateur groups were appearing everywhere. Curiously enough, it seems that the stage is a place where the Finns, usually so introverted, can truly give vent to their feelings.

Nowadays there are some forty professional theatres in the country, the northernmost being in Rovaniemi, north of the Arctic Circle. Public subsidies have kept the theatre accessible to the whole nation; indeed, in this country of five million people almost three million theatre tickets are sold every year.

On average, about half the performances are of works by Finnish playwrights. The perennial favourites include the plays of Aleksis Kivi, Minna Canth (1844–1897), Maria Jotuni (1880–1943) and the Estonian-born Hella Wuolijoki (1886–1954), usually set among well-to-do farmers or the educated gentry.

New winds began to blow in the 1960s, particularly in the productions of independent theatre groups. Directors like Kalle Holmberg (b. 1939), Ralf Långbacka (b. 1932), Jouko Turkka (b. 1942) and Arto af Hällström (b. 1952) also went on to challenge the established tenets of institutional theatre. The big theatres are not afraid to take risks nowadays, although from time to time they must of course resort to popular hits to stay afloat.

The contemporary style emphasizes visual and physical elements. A certain distance from the dramatic heritage is cultivated in updated versions of the classics. Recent examples include a silent version of one of Minna Canth's well-loved Finnish rural dramas; performances by an all-female cast of Aeschylus, Shakespeare and Gogol; and stylized analyses of Dostoevskyan guilt or Tolstoyan ethics. A boldly experimental approach has infused these performances with new forcefulness and vitality.

Finland has a major international theatre forum in the Tampere Theatre. A summer event first held in 1968, it took on a new lease of life in the late eighties when Vivica Bandler, the *grande dame* of the Finnish theatre world and a tireless innovator, took over as artistic director.

Film

It is not easy to be a filmmaker in a country the size of Finland. Without government support, it would be virtually impossible, for very few films indeed can attract one hundred thousand viewers – the number required to turn a profit – in a country with a population of five million. And obviously Finnish films must rely on Finnish audiences.

Nonetheless, the Finnish film industry has survived, though on a modest scale. Ten films or so are now made in an average year, as against fifteen in the heady '80s.

The big commercial hits tend to be farces such as the *Uuno Turhapuro* films by Spede Pasanen (1930–2001). The Finns also love film versions of their literary classics, especially the war novels *Tuntematon sotilas* (The

◄ In his street theatre performance at the opening of the Tampere Theatre Festival, Reijo Kela wound up on a treetop.

Unknown Soldier) by Väinö Linna (1920–1992) and *Talvisota* (The Winter War) by Antti Tuuri (b. 1944). The director Markku Pölönen (b. 1957) has won the Finns' hearts with his explorations of the Finnish mentality and the country's recent history, especially in *Kuningasjätkä* (Summer by the River). Renny Harlin (b. 1959) has made a career in Hollywood with films of action, horror and adventure, but has not had much success in his home country.

Among the currently active directors, the Kaurismäki brothers Aki (b. 1957) and Mika (b. 1955) have been particularly successful in Europe. Especially the cinephiles of France, Germany and Britain take pleasure in the extreme stylization, quiet irony and tragicomic humanist outlook of the Kaurismäkis' films.

The characters they love to depict are anti-heroes: lost, lonely, silent

▲ The film *Valkoinen peura* (The White Reindeer) by Erik Blomberg from 1952 is the story of a Lapp witch. The main themes are the mystique of Lapland, all-consuming love and jealousy.

THE KAURISMÄKI BROTHERS

■ The opening in 1982 of Mika Kaurismäki's (b. 1955) first feature film, *Arvottomat* (The Worthless), marked a milestone in the history of Finnish cinema: the slow, deliberately artificial speech, the stilted phrases, understated gestures and expressions and general use of clichés represented a new approach to filmmaking in Finland.

Later the director has tried his hand at more traditional films. Although *Rosso* (1985) is another story of an aimless wanderer, *Amazon* (1990), filmed in South America, takes a clear stand in favour of the rainforest and the global environment.

Aki Kaurismäki (b. 1957) started his career in cinema as scriptwriter and assistant director for his older brother. In his own feature films, he has developed an even more pronounced stylization, with a strong sense of tradition and a curiously oblique humour. Several of his films have attained the status of modern classics: *Varjoja paratiisissa* (Shadows in Paradise, 1986), *Tulitikkutehtaan tyttö* (The Match Factory Girl, 1990), *Kauas pilvet karkaavat* (Drifting Clouds, 1996) – already something of an international hit – and *Mies vailla menneisyyttä* (The Man Without a Past, 2002). The last-mentioned film garnered the Grand Prix in Cannes as well as the Best Actress prize for Kati Outinen.

▶ Aki Kaurismäki is Finland's most successful film director. Released in 2002, *Mies vailla menneisyyttä* (The Man Without a Past) has won numerous international awards, including the Grand Prix of the jury at the Cannes Film Festival. The lead roles are played by Markku Peltola and Kati Outinen.

▲ Rauni Mollberg directed a pacifist
adaptation of Väinö Linna's classic novel
The Unknown Soldier.

tramps who prefer the role of the per-
petual loser to that of the glib yuppy.
Despite the critical praise showered
on them, the Kaurismäkis' films rarely
reach a large audience; they are cult
movies cherished by small groups of
connoisseurs.

Pirjo Honkasalo (b. 1947) has received numerous awards for her docu-
mentaries, including *Atman*, filmed in
India. Her feature film *Tulennielijä*
(Fire Eater) has also won acclaim in
Finland and abroad. Honkasalo received the Finnish Art Award in 1998.

Auli Mantila (b. 1964) follows in
the Kaurismäkis' footsteps, but has
perhaps an even more uncompro-
misingly detached, spare style. Her
first full-length feature film, *Neitoperho*
(The Collector) already won international recognition. It is in the form of
a horror film, presenting a cheerless vision of modern man's spiritual home-
lessness and longing for love, building
up to a powerful ethical statement. In

Pelon maantiede (The Geography of
Fear) Mantila depicts the fear and violence arising from society's lack of respect for human dignity.

Despite these notable contributions, the true golden age of Finnish
film was back in the 1930s, a period
that saw a whole spate of directors
and actors who have taken on an
aura of legend. Before his early death
in the Winter War, Nyrki Tapiovaara
(1911–1940) made cool, stylized film
versions of the classics of Finnish literature, to which the bold, melodra-
matic effects of Teuvo Tulio (b. 1912)
stood in complete contrast. Valentin
Vaala (1909–1976) directed no less
than 44 films; his register ranged from
comedy to thriller and from folk drama to literary classic.

One of the most notable Finnish
filmmakers of the latter half of
the 20th century is Rauni Mollberg
(b. 1929). His *Maa on syntinen laulu*
(The Earth is a Sinful Song) won international acclaim. Set in the remote
backwoods of Lapland, this primitive
love story conjured up a fierce vision
of nature, sex, religion and guilt. Mollberg also directed a remake of Linna's

great war novel, *The Unknown Soldier.*
This was a daring enterprise considering that the earlier film, directed by
Edvin Laine (1905–89), had come to
be regarded as the definitive screen
version. Mollberg succeeded in his in-
tention of stirring up controversy, for
his pacifist interpretation presented
the Finnish soldier, not as a quick-
witted hero, but as a sensitive, vulnerable youth, little more than a child.
Buffeted by war and at the mercy of
the vast, subarctic forest, the helpless-
ness of the human condition takes on
mythic proportions.

Literature

Inspired by the National Romantic
movement in the nineteenth century,
the Finns raised literature to a pedestal
even higher than that of art: it showed
the nation the path to be followed,
symbolizing the country's independent
existence. It held up a mirror to show
who we were and where we came from.
Since the reflection was not always flat-
tering, bitter literary wars broke out
from time to time.

For many centuries, since the
time of Finland's first writer known
by name, the monk Jöns Budde
(c. 1437– c. 1491), most of Finland's
literature was written in either Swedish
or Latin. It took a long time before
a vernacular literature was created, although Finnish as a written language
had existed since the Reformation,
when Mikael Agricola (c. 1510–1557)
published an ABC and translated the
New Testament and other works into
Finnish in the 1540s.

▲ The original Finnish edition of the novel
Sinuhe the Egyptian by Mika Waltari.

▼ Illustration by Erkki Tanttu to Aleksis
Kivi's novel *The Seven Brothers.*

Only in the nineteenth century did Finnish literature really come into its own. J.L. Runeberg (1804–1877), who wrote in Swedish, created a poetic, idealized image of the Finnish peasantry as a pious and brave folk. Aleksis Kivi (1834–1872), who wrote in Finnish, saw his people in a more realistic and humorous light. His novel *Seitsemän veljestä* (The Seven Brothers) is still far and away the most popular classic of Finnish literature.

The electronic media represent a powerful rival to literature these days. Nonetheless, the Finns are still among the world's most voracious readers. In an average year, more books are published per capita in Finland than in

KALEVALA

■ Elias Lönnrot (1802–1884) published two seminal compilations of folk poetry, the epic *Kalevala* (1835) and the lyric *Kanteletar* (1840), both received with great excitement throughout the country – although the first readers could not make much of the difficult language, the educated classes being mainly Swedish-speaking.

The poems of the *Kalevala* are in trochaic tetrameter, a poetic measure believed to have originated some two thousand years ago. There is no rhyme, but regular refrains and alliteration serve as props for the memory. The language is lively and the characters are portrayed with care. Educators have been prompt to point out that the most important battles in the epic are waged with words rather than swords.

In fact the *Kalevala* is a distinctly feminine epic. The principal theme is human relations: love and sex, wooing and marriage. The women are strong, the men often weak and pathetic. And yet the epic also contrived to offer the Finns the heroes they craved. Especially the wise old Väinämöinen represents a model for spiritual values.

Far more folk poetry has survived than could be fitted into the two early collections. When the entire corpus was compiled and published between 1908 and 1948 as *Suomen kansan vanhat runot* (The ancient poetry of the Finnish people), the material filled 33 volumes.

The *Kalevala* has provided an inspiration for later folklore studies, too. In recent years, ethnographers have recorded modern culture, children's traditions, workplace traditions, war memories, urban stories and customs. The Finnish Literature Society's folk poetry archives – the world's largest of their kind – comprise some three million recorded poems. In the early 1990s, someone counted that the manuscripts alone filled 474 metres of bookshelves, in addition to which the archives have recordings and videos.

Especially during the nineteenth century, the *Kalevala* aroused an enormous enthusiasm for national culture among Finland's artists, designers, architects, composers and writers. They made long journeys on foot to the eastern parts of the country and as far as the villages of Russian Karelia. With the new millennium, folk poetry is coming into its own again. The heroes of the *Kalevala* march across the stage in Finnish drama and opera. CD-ROMs, strip cartoons and world music based on *Kalevala* themes are cropping up apace in Finland and elsewhere, too. The Helsinki heavy metal band *Amorphis* is making a name for itself with rock music based on folk poetry. An album called *Tales from the Thousand Lakes*, likewise based on the Kalevala, has sold some one hundred thousand copies in Germany and the United States.

Indeed, it is our ethnic music that has probably gained most new friends. New folk song and instrumental ensembles keep appearing, some of the best-known being *Tallari*, *Värttinä*, *Me naiset* and *Loituma*. Even the venerable national instrument, the *kantele*, has been dusted off and been given a new lease of life.

any other country. Most Finnish writers today use the Finnish language, but some write in Swedish and a handful in Sámi.

Things are not easy for Finnish writers: there are only five million speakers of Finnish, and Finnish books face a prohibitively high language barrier. All the same, an ever-increasing number of books manage to cross that barrier. The all-time international hit is the historical novel *Sinuhe egyptiläinen* (Sinuhe the Egyptian) by Mika Waltari (1908–1979), translated into 32 languages, which has cropped up on bestseller lists in various countries.

Friends of early 20th century poetry are familiar with the name of Edith

▶ Finnish artists have been inspired by the *Kalevala* for over a century now. Particularly impressive were the illustrations by Akseli Gallen-Kallela. Hannu Väisänen discovered in the folk epic a heady mix of violence and aesthetics. The photo shows Väisänen's work *The Gold Cloth of the Maid of Pohja*: "Busy weaving cloth of gold, / Carefully the silver threading, / Weaving with a golden shuttle, / And a weaver's reed of silver."

The annual review for this music is the Kaustinen Folk Music Festival, which started out in the 1960s as a showcase for the local fiddlers, but is now a megafestival of world music, attracting thousands of performers and one hundred thousand visitors to this small Ostrobothnian town every summer.

ADVENTURE IN MOOMIN VALLEY

■ Adventure and homecoming, friendship and solitude, the braving of danger and the warmth of the family hearth are the classic ingredients of Tove Jansson's storybook world. The combination of genuine fairytale and insightful character portrayal have made Jansson's books perennial favourites of children and adults alike.

Tove Jansson was born 1914 in Helsinki, the daughter of an artistic family. She studied painting, and invented the Moomintroll figure in the 1940s. The first Moomin book, *Kometjakten*, (Comet in Moominland) was published in 1945 with the writer's own illustrations. Jansson went on to publish a dozen other Moomin books as well as several novels and short stories for grown-up readers.

Nowadays the Moomin books are available in several dozen languages, and the Moomins have even ventured as far afield as Japanese animated films for television.

△ Tove Jansson at the time she created the Moomins. In her hand is Moominmamma with her handbag, with several Moominpapas and Moomintrolls and the Snorkmaiden on the table.

THE FINN'S FAVOURITE HAUNT: THE LIBRARY

■ In the 1990s the Finns have broken virtually all the world records connected to public libraries. Finland has the highest number of registered borrowers, approximately one half of the population. The number of loans in proportion to the population is likewise high, some twenty books a year. The number of library visits – some six million a year – is also proportionally the world's highest.

The Finnish library network is exceptionally efficient and covers the whole country. Bookmobiles carry books even to the smallest villages hidden away in the vast forests. All the same, small municipal libraries, in particular, were hard hit by the recession of the early 1990s, although during it the number of users increased by ten per cent, and more in places. Although the number of foreign-language videos and works of poetry has had to be cut, lending is still free of charge.

▶ Mobile libraries serve readers in fringe areas. The Helsinki City Library received an award in 1998 for "The Most Beautiful Bookmobile".

Södergran (1892–1923), a Finn who wrote poetry in Swedish. This shy, consumptive but fiercely individualistic young woman arrived at a revolutionary free verse form independently at about the same time as Ezra Pound and T.S. Eliot in English.

Among the modernist poets of the 1950s, the outstanding figures were Paavo Haavikko (b. 1931), Eeva-Liisa Manner (1921–1995), Bo Carpelan (b. 1926), Veijo Meri (b. 1928) and Pentti Saarikoski (1937–1983). More recently, a racy northern exoticism, coupled with a longing for freedom, has found expression in the prose of Arto Paasilinna (b. 1942) and Rosa Liksom (b. 1958). The *Moomin* books of Tove Jansson (1914–2001) are international classics of children's literature.

The Midsummer writers' congress in Lahti has provided a biennial forum for East-West dialogue since the late 1960s.

▲ Pentti Saarikoski, an outstanding poet and translator – and the *enfant terrible* of his day.

The Finnish media

Compared with the United States, European countries have tended towards a higher degree of government control of the media. Even Europe, however, has had a great variety of arrangements for ownership and control, ranging from full government control to an American-type decentralized media system. Finland has had perhaps the most decentralized communication system in Europe.

The Finns are exceptional media users. In most developed countries, TV viewing has increased, while reading has decreased. Not so in Finland: since the introduction of television in the 1950s, the number of newspapers, periodicals and books published has increased, and so has their readership.

Contrary to most other countries, television viewing has increased very slowly in Finland since the early 1960s,

and average viewing time is among the lowest in the industrial countries. The Americans watch 2.5 times as much TV as the Finns, and the British and Japanese about double the Finns' two hours a day. This despite the fact that in Finland the number of TV sets per family is among the highest in the world. Moreover, for a European country, Finland has a large number of TV channels offering a wide variety of programmes.

The Finnish press has always been privately owned. The Finns are great newspaper readers. If we combine all the international statistics on reading – newspapers, periodicals, books and library services – the Finns are world champions.

The leading communication company is SanomaWSOY, the publisher of *Helsingin Sanomat*, one of the leading newspapers in Scandinavia. The same company also publishes the evening paper *Ilta-Sanomat*, as well as a number of periodicals and magazines. It also owns WSOY (Finland's largest book publisher), the Channel 4 television network and Helsinki Television, which operates the country's largest cable TV system.

Magazine publishers include Yhtyneet Kuvalehdet, a large group owned by Otava Publishing Company; the group is now called Otava-Kuvalehdet Oy. Among other Finnish publishing companies, Tammi now belongs to the Swedish group Bonniers. Otava and Gummerus are family-owned publishing houses. The Finns are avid readers, of books as well as of newspapers and magazines. Unlike most other countries, newspapers and magazines are generally sold by subscription.

Broadcasting operations were started in Finland by radio amateurs in the 1920s. The first radio companies were all private. In 1934 the government-controlled Finnish Broadcasting Company (Yleisradio Ab or YLE) was formed from an existing private company, and it bought up all the other private companies. The country never actually had a statutory radio or TV monopoly, although between 1933 and 1955 YLE was the only player in the broadcasting business. Since 1955 there have again been several competing broadcasting enterprises.

In 1955 students of the Helsinki University of Technology set up a private TV company called TESVISIO. A year later YLE started TV broadcasts, sharing its channel with another private company, Oy MTV Ab. In 1963 YLE bought up TESVISIO. New private TV companies have been established since 1995. In 2000 there were two national channels operated by YLE and the private channels MTV3 (which has nothing to do with the international music channel MTV) and Channel 4, which is owned by SanomaWSOY. Cable television was introduced in Finland in the early 1970s. Most of the companies were small local cable systems. There are some more extensive systems, however, the largest being the Helsinki systems owned by SanomaWSOY.

In addition to the YLE network of radio stations, there are numerous private radio companies. Their number varies with shifting business fortunes, but is typically between 40 and 60. They are nearly all financed by advertisers; there are only a couple of small non-commercial private radio stations. Finnish broadcasting technology has always been in the forefront of development. YLE was one of the first companies to adopt FM radio after the Second World War, and it has now entered a new digital age in radio and TV services.

◄ Finland has a wide range of newspapers, published in Finnish or in Swedish. On average, 12–69-year-olds spend 8 hours 30 minutes per week following the media.

Index

Photographs